Retiring
SOLO

**Plan To Be Happy,
Healthy and Independent
in the Years Ahead**

By Lori Martinek

herlife
publishing, LLC

Published by Herlife Publishing LLC

Published by Herlife Publishing LLC
Order additional copies at www.herlifepublishing.com

Retiring Solo. Plan To Be Happy, Healthy and Independent in the
Years Ahead

For information on foreign, translation or other rights, please contact:
Herlife Publishing LLC
www.herlifepublishing.com

Contact Lori Martinek at
www.encorebusinessadvisors.com

Cover Design: Cindy Miller Design
Interior design and production: Cindy Miller Design
Author Photography: Babe Sarver

Printed in the United State of America

Solo means one.

As a noun, it is something done by one person, unaccompanied. As a verb, it means to accomplish something on your own. Solo does not mean alone, isolated or lonely.
Never did, never will.

Retirement typically implies the end of something, such as a job or a career. When we say that we are 'retiring' from something, we imply that we are about to be done. To retire also means to go to bed, to rest, to stop for a while. The new retirement is about none of these things. It is about beginnings rather than endings, and the active pursuit of true interests and passions over a period of time which, given modern life expectancies, could be decades long.

To Retire Solo means to individually plan for and pursue a balanced, active life which fulfills our interests while also helping us remain independent as we age. It is about being responsible for ourselves (one), navigating a successful life transition from one stage to another (retirement), and creating a sense of community that will help us continue to live independent and socially active lives as we grow older.

Now that we've got all of that straight, let's proceed.

Table of Contents

Foreword

Solo is much more than just a status or a state of mind. Each of us is born solo and each of us will spend much of our lives solo. Often, we will also die solo. Most of us, in fact, are likely to spend much, if not most, of our lives as solos – whether through choice, circumstances or a little bit of both.

As a nation, we are becoming increasingly solo and decidedly more solo-minded. The number of solos is increasing with each passing year. For the first time in U.S. history, the number of American singles outnumbers the number of married individuals. Many American are opting not to marry, or to structure their relationships in less traditional ways. Those who do marry are choosing to tie the knot at a later age. At the same time, the U. S. divorce rate is lower than it has been in decades. Is there a connection between the two trends? It could be that there is less divorce because fewer people are choosing to get married in the first place. Is being solo becoming more socially acceptable as it becomes more common? And, if so, are even more people likely to embrace being solo in the future?

According to a June 2016 *TIME* magazine cover article entitled '*How to Stay Married*', marriage is 'the most basic and intimate of our social institutions, but also the one most subject to shifts in cultural, technological and economic forces, many of which have made single life a completely viable and attractive proposition'. The author missed an opportunity to explore that statement more fully. Exactly why are so many people choosing to be single, stay single or get single these days? That's the cultural shift that should be examined more fully.

Perspectives on why people choose to be or remain solo are often a reflection of age. Retirement, perhaps even mid-life, is the time when being solo begins to 'come into its own'. No one really expects you to pair up again (or for the first time) one you get past 'a certain age'. The pressure to 'couple up' dies down. People who have spent their whole lives being solo no longer appear to be renegades. Singlism, as social psychologist Bella DePaulo calls the discrimination that many singles face throughout their lives, seems to lessen – at least the societal aspects of it (the economic discrepancies continue). Society seems to be much more comfortable with the concept of an 'older' solo person. We are growing more accustomed to seeing older people on their own and living alone, many of them by choice. They seem to be everywhere, and they seem to be pretty darn happy.

People are also living longer and are staying healthier for more of their lives. Because of that, many of them are choosing to retire later, or to pursue second careers. Finances are also a factor. Most Americans are more worried about whether they will outlive their money or whether they can afford to retire in the first place. The good news is that we can expect to live longer, sometimes well into our 90's. The bad news is that we will have to save more money to cover the costs of living that long. Many (really most) Americans are financially unprepared for retirement, often woefully so, and they are realizing that, unless the U.S. social services system (Social Security, Medicare and general healthcare, et al) expands in a very significant way, they will have to continue working beyond the traditional retirement age of 65 and well into their 70's.

This is a book about retiring solo, and not just about ageing or retirement. Single people have always had to work harder to be able to put away money for retirement, primarily because they must live off of one income, their own, while covering 100 percent of their housing costs and other living expenses. All of this can make it very difficult to save for retirement or build an emergency fund for unexpected expenses. Solos living on their own also lack the 'contingency plans' that married couples or partnered solos often have access to. There is no second person with a second income to pick up the slack economically if a job is lost or an unexpected expense crops up.

Solos have to plan harder for retirement and start earlier. They need to consider where and how they will live, how they will make sure that they have a support system in place if their health fails or something goes wrong, and how they will stay active and socially engaged as they get older. Finding and nurturing a sense of community is essential for everyone. As humans, we want and need to feel as if we are part of a community, at least on some basic level. These days, that sense of community, and the support system which often comes with it, is as likely to come from friends, co-workers, activity partners or housemates as it is from a spouse or significant other. Community building is one area where solos often excel.

There's no doubt that retirement is different for solos, but not all of the differences are challenges. We're only just beginning to discover how satisfied and happy many older solos really are. They are active and engaged, and leading lives that are busy with work, activities or volunteering. Many of them try out new careers or pursue new passions. Active older solos often find that being on their own allows them to sample and make a greater range of life choices that truly reflect their interests and talents.

Solos also enjoy greater flexibility and freedom than their coupled counterparts when it comes to planning. They have the ability to make plans based on their needs and preferences. Their retirement strategies are more likely to reflect where and how they want to live and how they want to save and spend their money. Their lives, perhaps for the first time, become focused on what *they* want to do and how *they* want to spend their time. This can be very empowering.

The topics in this book will be relevant to anyone – whether solo or married, partnered or otherwise paired off. Why? Because everyone who isn't solo right now is likely to become solo again at some point. That's the reality. We begin our lives as solos and we typically also end them that way. Planning for a solo retirement is a practical, proactive choice, no matter how coupled and happy you may be at this moment. Why? You wouldn't want to find yourself suddenly on your own without a financial plan, a housing strategy and a support system in place as you get older. No one does. If you are already solo, you know this, you've thought about it and you've hopefully starting creating a plan. If you're not solo, you need to start thinking about the very real possibility that you will be solo again at some point in the future and then begin planning for that time. This book will put the possibilities (and the issues) on your radar, regardless of your current status, and get you thinking about how you want to live your life and what it will take for you to realize that goal, financially, physically and socially. It will give you a framework to begin making preliminary decisions and plans now, so that you can create the best retirement experience possible.

The 'new retirement' is a concept that has no real definition or boundaries. It is more about rebalancing, reimagining, reinventing and rebooting than about retiring from a lifetime of work. It is time to think of planning for retirement as a collective *re-thinking* of what we want in our lives and how we want to spend our time.

I was nearing my Beddian birthday before I finally embraced my solo-ness. (Your Beddian birthday is the one in which you become the age that matches the last two digits of the year in which you were born. I was born in 1958 and I turned 58 while I was writing this book.) It was during the year leading up to that milestone that I realized two important things: 1) Being single and living solo is what works best for me, and 2) Because of that, I need to take full responsibility for my financial future. Once you make the decision that you don't want to get married again (or perhaps ever), you must also accept the mantle of providing for your own 'happily ever after'. I came to this realization quite willingly. Others may finally accept it after years of unsuccessfully trying to find a partner or spouse. In either situation, 'the bucks stop here', at your front door. No one is going to provide for your future, or even help provide for your future, except you – which, if you think about it, is the way that it should be anyway. As daunting as that might seem on the surface, it's actually a very empowering realization to accept.

I have always worked hard to put money away for my far away future retirement. At the same time, and until very recently, I assumed that there would eventually be another partner or spouse in my life – someone who would likely share expenses in the future. It's still possible that I could find myself in a committed relationship at some point, but it's highly unlikely that I would consider marriage or living with someone again. I really do love my solo lifestyle. It took me a long time to realize how well it suits me.

Once I realized how happy and satisfied I was with my life and lifestyle, I stopped trying to 'couple up' in a traditional sense. I took charge and committed to actively planning for a solo future. It has been very, very empowering. The 'bag lady syndrome' that I had suffered from throughout my career has finally gone away. I gained confidence in my ability to provide for myself. I've got this.

I did have a little experience to work with. I have been divorced three times and, through one of those divorces, lost two retirement funds – one to a bad divorce settlement and the second to establish college funds for my two children, also the result of that settlement. Losing the first fund wiped out years of saving. Losing the second put my savings back another eight years. I am currently building my third retirement fund. When I think of where I could have been at this point if I had been stronger (and had hired a better lawyer), I get frustrated, but there's no changing history – only learning from it.

I've learned some other things along the way. In the five years before I embraced being solo, I had several opportunities to 'marry money', as in a significant amount of money. On all three occasions, I chose not to. Money should never be a reason to get married or to compromise your life in any way. Financial security should never be a reason to 'couple up'. One of things that I worked very hard to teach my daughter, and to impart to any woman whom I have mentored or known, is how important it is to create your own financial independence. (I am talking about financial independence, not wealth.) Economic independence (e.g. earning your own money) will always allow you to be able to make decisions from a position of strength, and not from financial need. Nothing is more empowering.

Retirement is no different. Whether you are about to be married, involved in a long-term, committed relationship or satisfied with your strong solo self, it is up to you – and only you – to plan for your financial future. All of us, male and female, will be solo at some point: whether again, for the first time in a long time or gloriously still. Solo retirement is in everyone's future. Be powerful as well as practical and plan for it.

Solo Retirement: Charting a Course to a Bright, Independent Future

Millions of Americans are finding themselves on their own as they head toward retirement. Some are solo by circumstances, others by choice. Baby Boomers all of them, they are driving new trends in housing, work, caretaking and traveling, while also redefining what it means to be part of a community. These partner-less pioneers are rewriting the book on retirement as they learn what it takes to successfully retire solo and remain happy, healthy and independent in the coming years.

Solo Statistics

Solos face special challenges when it comes to retirement. Everything – including planning, saving and spending – rests solely on their shoulders. They and only they are responsible for what their retirement years will look like.

Each year, nearly two million single people reach the age of 65, a milestone which would have made them 'ripe' for retirement in the past. People nearing that milestone today do not feel financially prepared to retire. They realize that they may have to continue working or come up with another source of income to supplement their Social Security benefits. Many have not really thought about how they will spend their time in retirement after the first few months or how or where they may want to live. Most hope to maintain their current standard of living or even improve on it by traveling and pursuing new interests. It is unlikely that will happen unless their finances improve. Those who are married are probably counting on their spouse's income to help save for retirement and to provide a second Social Security check. Statistics, however, indicate that many of these Boomers are likely to become solo in the future.

In short, there are no guarantees and safety nets are few and far between in almost everyone's retirement outlook. Baby Boomers, however, have always been game changers. From the start, the generation that was born between 1946 and 1964 has rewritten rules and policies, fought for social change and proved itself to be a fast learner, a trend setter, a problem solver and a culture creator. Financial security, success, status and a sense of belonging have always been important to the post-WWII generation, as has independence and personal freedom. There is no indication that ageing Baby Boomers expect – or want – retirement to be any different. I know this because I'm one of them. Now we just have to figure out how to make that happen.

A 2014 Bloomberg analysis of U.S. Census data from 2012 reported that there were 124.6 million people over the age of 16 – or roughly 50.2 percent of the U.S. population – who were single. For the first time since 1976 (when data tracking began), single persons outnumbered married folks in America, according to the Bloomberg report.

There were just over 40 million adults age 65 and older in 2014, representing 13 percent of the U.S. population. That percentage will continue to increase until it reaches 20 percent in 2030, when the entire Baby Boomer generation will be 65 or older. America is getting older. Much older.

The same census data revealed that single persons made up more than half of the population in 27 of the 50 states and that 34 million people (28 percent of the population) were living alone. That percentage was up from 17 percent in 1970. The data also showed that 46 percent of all U.S. households were run by a single person, though all of those individuals were not necessarily living alone. Many were committed singles living together or non-related solos living in various types of arrangements. According to the data, about 12 percent of unmarried adults ages 50 through 64 were living together but not married in 2012, which was up from the 7 percent reported in 2000. America is not only getting older, but more single.

A Pew Research Center 2014 analysis of the 2012 census data found that, since 1970, there has been a steady increase in the share of the U.S. population that remains 'never married' by the time they reach 45 to 54 years old. About 20 percent of all singles over the age of 25 (roughly 42 million people) had never been married. It further suggested that, based on the above statistic and a combination of choice and circumstances, 25 percent of all Millennials (defined as those who were born roughly between 1981 and 1997 and also known as the 'echo generation') will likely never get married. In 2015, they numbered 75.3 million adults and, for the first time, surpassed Baby Boomers (74.9 million adults ages 51 to 69) as the largest living generation. The number of solos in the U.S. is expected to continue increasing from this point forward due to cultural shifts that were pioneered by Baby Boomers and are now being carried on by the Millennials who follow them.

It appears that these singles are leading full lives, are happy with their lifestyle and enjoying their independence without regret. A 2006 survey by the Pew Internet and American Life Project found that 55 percent of the never-married had zero interest in seeking a romantic partner. They also reported that they are far less lonely or isolated than people may think. Studies have shown that single men and women tend to be more social and involved in their community than married couples, who often 'turn inward' after coupling up. Childless solos also tend to provide more time and support to parents, family and friends than their married counterparts.

Solos tend to vote and their numbers are growing. Unmarried persons made up 39 percent of all voters in the 2012 election. Solos also tend to be educated. Eighty-seven percent of all unmarried adults 25 and older had a high school or higher education in 2014. Nearly 30 percent of that same demographic had earned a Bachelor's degree or higher.

Solo is no longer just 'a stop' on the way to 'a happy ending'. For many, it's a lifestyle choice and, often, the destination. For some, it's an unexpected development or the unavoidable result of growing older. The reality is that most Americans will spend more time solo than in a married or committed relationship over their lifetimes. Solo is a natural, dynamic state that we experience as we cycle in and out of life stages, living arrangements and relationships. We will all find ourselves solo at some point and for many of us – and women especially – it is likely to be our status as we navigate the later years of life. Whether being solo is a lasting or intermittent part of any one person's life, it is definitely a reality of the modern landscape.

What It Means To Be Solo

So what does it mean to be solo these days, and why am I calling it solo instead of single? The word 'single' carries a lot of baggage with it. It implies 'not married', only one or alone – none of which define the concept well. The reality is that, today, marriage is a destination for only part of the U.S. population. More households are being created around non-traditional families and/or living arrangements than ever before. And: Solos are rarely alone and far from lonely. Research, in fact, shows that they are typically more social and involved in the community than married couples, who tend to focus more on their own relationship, and less on the world around them once they have 'coupled up'.

In the book, *On My Own*, author Florence Falk calls it 'aloneness' and writes that 'aloneness has been and will continue to be an overlooked and undervalued dimension of (our) lives, one we will all experience and owe it to ourselves to learn about'. Falk stressed that 'aloneness' is not the same as 'loneliness'. Rather, it is an opportunity 'for growth and transformation'; a way to learn about ourselves, what we need and what we are capable of. Well said.

Sociologists and census takers seem to prefer the term 'unmarried', which works as a far-reaching umbrella for different categories of singles who might be parents or childless, living alone or with one or more partners, be widowed or divorced or any combination of the above. But again, using the term 'unmarried' implies that marriage is the goal – or at least the barometer against which all other types of relationships should be measured. It is not.

It's time to change the terminology. Solo is a stronger word. It is straightforward and non-editorial. It applies to one person, regardless of their living situation. It is empowering. It fits.

And that's because the stigma is disappearing from being solo or living solo. Solo has become a sign of independence and a destination in its own right. People who are solo by choice report that they are happy and proud to be solo. Long-held beliefs that married adults are happier than solo adults no longer ring true. Happiness is generally a factor of who we are (personality and genetics), not who we are with – though there's no doubt that being with the wrong person can certainly make a person very unhappy.

More adults are also choosing to live solo while creating a sense of community around themselves. They enjoy the independence, the freedom and the privacy of living alone, but also like knowing that there are friends and potential activity partners nearby. Solo living is coming into its own and we will take a closer look at emerging housing options in a later chapter.

Solo is an umbrella that encompasses a number of different categories. They include:

- Solo by Choice
- Solo by Circumstances
- Solo by Chance
- Suddenly Solo
- Potentially Solo

Each of us will fit into one or more of these subsets during our lifetimes, sometimes more than once. Everyone is Potentially Solo at any time, no matter how happily paired up they may feel or be at this moment.

Solo by Choice applies to long-time solos who have made a conscious decision to be solo and are happy with their choice.

A growing number of Baby Boomers and Millennials fit into this category. For them, solo is a lifestyle. They may be delaying marriage or partnership, or never planning on it. They may be living alone or with others. In any event, they are content and they are not going to give up their solo status lightly. They expect – and likely have begun planning – to grow older and ultimately retire as a solo.

Social psychologist Bella DePaulo calls this 'single at heart' (which is also the name of her online column at *Psych Central*). How do you know if you are single at heart? According to DePaulo, your life 'may or may not include the occasional romantic relationship and you may or may not live alone or want to live alone, but you don't aspire to live as part of a couple (married or otherwise) for the long term'. You can be single at heart regardless of your actual status as single or coupled, she adds.

Whether Solo by Choice or 'single at heart', you're likely to be self-sufficient and comfortable with your own company. Single life feels natural. It's where you do your best work. Or as DePaulo wrote: 'My sense so far is that for people who are single at heart, once they get past the cultural expectations about what they should be doing, and maybe their own internalization of the prevailing ideology that says that everyone wants to marry and that's the only way to be truly happy, they recognize something profound: Single life suits them. It is a life they embrace. It feels right and true.'

That's a perfect description of my journey, which took me through multiple marriages and motherhood before I realized that I am 'single at heart'. I have always done my best work and been my most creative when I am between relationships. Why? Because when I am single I use my time and energy to plan, do, dare and dream. A pleaser and a caretaker by nature, my social life also soars when I am not in a relationship where I am focused on the needs or schedule of a partner. Ditto on my community involvement and service. I have more time to give freely when the only schedule that I have to consider is my own. Solo is where I am the most powerful, the most creative and the most giving. It is likely how I will choose to spend the rest of my life.

Solo by Circumstance includes people who may be solo due to career or education demands, family responsibilities (an increasing number of Baby Boomers are finding themselves in a caretaker role) or economics. For others, it might be a factor of sexuality or transition (life, gender or geography). Solo may be more of a life phase for people in this category – some of whom may be planning to 'partner up' at some point. Others will ultimately embrace the solo life, after having had an opportunity to experience it. Solo by Circumstance is the category which many of us may fall into and out of over the years as we transition between relationships.

Then there is a category which I will call Solo by Chance, which includes people who are 'reluctantly' solo. These are the folks who are on their own but would prefer to be married or in a committed relationship. They might be divorced, widowed or never married, parents or childless. What they share is their search to find someone to love and to be with. They have been unsuccessful in achieving that goal and, at some point, may realize that they are likely headed toward a solo future. They have (reluctantly) learned how to live solo over the years, but probably have not planned for a solo retirement because they prefer to hope that it will not happen. Many of them still think that their 'luck' will change and that they will end up as part of a couple at some point. Regardless of how things work out, they still need to plan for an independent financial future. The bonus? Doing so will also make them a stronger partner if they do end up in a committed relationship at some point.

Suddenly Solo includes individuals who have lost a partner or spouse due to death, divorce or breakup. (Another author called the last category 'dumped' to make it three D's, but that seems harsh.) Sometimes a status change is expected – as in a long-term illness or a long, unhappy marriage – often it is entirely unanticipated. In any case, it can be a difficult category to navigate, especially when it was not planned for, or even within the realm of considered possibilities.

Suddenly Solo is the category where 'learning to be solo' becomes very important. It can be especially critical in cases of 'gray divorce', where couples divorce (or break up) after more than 20 years of marriage (or civil marriage or partnership) – and often to the complete surprise of one of the partners.

Long-term marriages are no safer than shorter ones. According to a 2013 study by the National Center for Marriage and Family Research at Bowling Green University, the divorce rate of people 50 or older has more than doubled since 1990 and the rate for the 65 and older crowd has more than tripled. Data suggests that one in every four people who get divorced today is over the age of 50 and that nearly one in 10 is 65 or older. Faced with longer life expectancies and the potential for decades in an unhappy relationship still ahead of them, an increasing number of couples are 'opting out' once their nest is empty. Baby Boomers are significantly more likely than previous generations to be divorced and entering their 'retirement years' alone. For these solos, learning how to live, socialize and take care of themselves, by themselves again – or sometimes for the first time – requires a refresher course and a solo retirement plan.

Ditto for the many Boomer women who will find themselves widows in retirement. Women who reach age 65 are expected to live an average of 21 years more. The Association for Financial Counseling and Planning Education predicts that seven out of 10 Boomer women will outlive their husbands. Many of these women could end up living as 'solo widows' for 15 to 20 years. They should be planning for that possibility, even if their husbands are completely healthy today. Their spouses would be prudent to do so as well. Becoming a widower late in life is certainly not uncommon.

Everyone is Potentially Solo at any time in their life. Regardless of whether you are married, partnered or otherwise in a committed relationship (or headed toward one), *life happens*. It is always possible that you could become solo in the future and it is practical to plan for that time. (It is no less romantic that using a pre-nuptial agreement to protect your future in the event of a divorce.) Many people who marry will still spend more than half of their adult lives as solos. And, despite the decline in the divorce rate, about 40 percent of marriages (first and subsequent) still end in divorce, transitioning both former spouses back into the solo category.

On the average, 80 to 90 percent of all women will be solely responsible for their personal and financial health at some point, if they aren't already. It makes good sense to begin planning for that eventuality now to ease the transition, and to avoid the financial hardship which often comes with a shift in status. The good news? Women in younger generations (and when I say this, I include my age group, which is the tail end of the Boomer generation), have been responsible for providing for themselves for many years, and often for most of their adult lives. Knowing how to earn, use and invest money are important life skills that women need to possess as much as – if not more so – than men, given our longer life spans. Adult women now spend much, if not most, of their lives as a solo – regardless of the circumstances. That's the new reality that everyone must consider and plan for.

When it comes to life skills, solos of either sex who have had to learn how to support themselves and pay the bills with only one income to work with are usually in a better position to navigate the waters of retirement. The greater retirement challenge that they face is finding ways to actively save for retirement while also paying the higher cost of being and living solo in America.

Regardless of what category they are in or how they got there, solos need a retirement plan that will maintain their quality of life, build community, protect their health and – perhaps most importantly – preserve their independence as they grow older. No one wants to rely on others for their financial well-being. No one wants to suffer from poor health. No one wants to end up in a nursing facility and no one wants to be without some type of support system to turn to when necessary. These are issues that affect all of us, as individuals, regardless of our status. Learning how to retire solo is practical knowledge that each of us must acquire so that we can put it to good use now, and as we grow older.

The good news: Being solo also means that you can make important decisions about your future on your own and choose what is best for you, without having to compromise or consider another person's preferences. You can choose how to save for retirement, including how much and for how long, how and where to live, the types of food you buy, cook and eat, and how you choose to be active and engaged in the community. Your plan is truly *your* plan. Your needs and wants take priority. You get to choose the destination (goal) and plan the journey (strategy) to get there.

Planning for a solo retirement is a smart, proactive life strategy for everyone, regardless of age, gender or relationship status. Whatever category any of us may be in right now, we are likely to spend much of our lives being solely responsible for ourselves. This book will help you create a vision and a plan for a successful solo retirement, even if you 1) don't expect to be on your own again, 2) feel secure in your current savings strategy, or 3) feel that retirement is too far in the future to worry about. Keep in mind that 'life happens' and that, at some point, so will retirement.

The New Reality: Retirement Is Changing

The new reality is that retirement is changing. Actually, it has already changed. Today it is more about transitions, rather than endings. Retirement is less of a one-time milestone and more of an ongoing journey or process.

People are living longer. The youngest Baby Boomers began turning 50 in 2014. The latest forecasts predict that the average Baby Boomer male will live to be 82.7 years old. The average Baby Boomer woman will make it 85.3 years. That's three to four years longer than the average life expectancy of the previous generation, and despite the reality that Baby Boomers suffer more from obesity, high cholesterol, diabetes and hypertension, and are far more drug dependent than their parents. Healthy Boomers who make it to 75 can expect to live to 86 if they are a man and 88 if they are a woman. Some insurance companies have begun to rate women with life expectancies as high as 100. Everything, of course, depends on a person's health, habits, family history and geography.

Not knowing how many years you have left makes it difficult to plan for retirement. How many years of money will you need? At what pace should you spend what you have put away? I will write more about this in the upcoming section on work and money. There really is no way to know for sure. You can take an online life expectancy quiz (or several) to get a feel for how long you may live, based on your current health, habits and family history. You can find a variety of free life expectancy calculators online. I have included websites for three of them in the appendix. Be prepared for the results to vary. I took three different quizzes and came up with three different life expectancies: 98, 97 and 88. That's a range of 30 to 40 years ahead of me (I am 58 as I write this) – which is a far cry from the expected 10 years of retirement (from 65 to 75 years old) that earlier generations planned for.

When people live longer, their money also has to last longer. It should be no surprise then that many Baby Boomers are also working longer. Pew Research calls them the 'Threshold Generation' – adults who are at the threshold of retirement – and reports that they are actively thinking about postponing retirement or even avoiding it completely.

According to the Pew Research Center's Social and Demographic Trends Project (2009), 52 percent of all adults ages 50 to 64 who were working full-time said that they might delay their retirement. Another 16 percent said that did not expect to ever stop working. That percentage is twice as high as reported by younger workers. The University of Michigan's Health and Retirement Study reinforced that data when it reported that roughly six out of 10 men and women of retirement age don't plan to leave the labor force when they leave their full-time career jobs. They may change jobs or work less, but they don't plan to stop working entirely.

The Middle-Income Boomer Retirement Gap: Savings, Education and Advice study surveyed 1,000 Americans aged 50 to 68 who had an annual household income between $25,000 and $100,000. Forty-five percent of the respondents were already retired. Nearly as many of those who were still working (43 percent) expected to retire later than 65, versus 16 percent who planned to retire before 65. Only 19 percent expected to be able to retire at 65. That's not surprising. Baby Boomers need more money to retire because they are going to live longer than previous generations did – up to a third longer, according to the National Center for Health Statistics, which reports that the life expectancy of a 65-year-old has grown by 37% since 1950. As we saw with the results of my life expectancy test, that's probably the reality that I face. In other words, good health requires a healthy savings plan to go with it.

Common sense also tells us that retiring at 65 just doesn't make sense anymore, given longer life expectancies. Example: If we enter the workforce at 22, plan to retire at 65 and expect to live until 100, we will effectively work for 43 years while trying to save for a retirement which could last 35 years or more. According to the *Future of Aging: Realizing the Potential of Longevity* published by the Milken Institute Center for the Future of Ageing, 'This proposition may be attainable for some, but is mathematically impossible for many. Clearly, the long-held notion of stopping work altogether and fully retiring at 65 is ripe for disruption.'

The 2008 – 2012 recession has had the greatest impact on many American retirement plans. Respondents who lost 40 percent or more of their investment nest eggs during that time were nearly twice as likely to say that they will delay retirement than those who hadn't lost significant money in the economic meltdown. Americans are known to be notoriously bad savers when it comes to retirement. The recession took many of them even further away from their goals, and a slower than expected recovery has made it difficult for many people to catch up.

Gender and race can also be a factor. Women said that they are likely to work longer. This could be due to income disparity, later entry into the workforce or a life events which changed their economic status, such as divorce or the death of a spouse (becoming Suddenly Solo). White respondents said that they planned to work longer than their Asian or African American counterparts. Income level appears to be less of a factor. Everyone it seems – with the exception of the very rich – is feeling less than financially ready for retirement.

Americans are also worried about whether Social Security will survive, in what form and for how long. There is similar uncertainty about Medicare and its survival. Many Boomers are also part of the 'sandwich generation' and they are struggling to meet the needs of ageing parents and adult children at the same time that they are trying to plan and save for their own retirement needs.

Boomers are more optimistic as the economy gains traction, but they still have a lot of ground to make up. A 2015 CareerBuilder survey reported that more than half (54 percent) of older workers said that they plan to keep working past the 'traditional' retirement age, just not for the same company. Some plan to work for income or insurance benefits, others to remain 'involved' or to avoid boredom. A little more than 16 percent said that they plan to quit their present job to pursue a dream job or a completely new career.

There is some improvement on the horizon. The *2016 Retirement Confidence Survey* by the Employee Benefit Research Institute interviewed 1,000 workers and 505 retirees in January 2016. Among the key findings: The percentage of workers who are 'very confident' that they will have enough money for a comfortable retirement has increased from 13 percent in 2013 to 21 percent this year (2016). Those who reported that they are 'somewhat confident' rose to 42 percent, meaning that 63 percent have some degree of confidence that they will be able to manage a comfortable retirement. Whether that confidence is well founded or not remains to be seen.

But enough with statistics. You get the idea. We're living longer and working longer. The good news is that people who delay retirement also have a lower risk of developing Alzheimer's or other forms of dementia. Working, in whatever form we may choose, helps to 'keep us young' and more alert – even as we grow older.

Gold watches, pensions and other safety nets are mostly a thing of the past. We have to rethink the way that we look at retirement and create our own financial, social and physical security. Solo or not, we all need to think about how we are going to balance work with life, passions with commitments and the needs of others with our own. We need to think about what we still want to do and achieve in life, and make plans to be able to realize those dreams. Think of it more as 'rebalancing' than retirement. This is an opportunity to reshape your life into what you would like it to be. There is no 'one size fits all' strategy or plan – and there shouldn't be. The myth of the 'average American' is just that: a myth. Your plan should be uniquely your own.

There are a lot of books and websites that focus on planning for retirement. Many are focused on the financial aspects: saving, investing and planning for your financial future. Most of them are geared toward couples or two-income families. Almost all of them ignore solos and non-traditional households.

This book focuses solely (pun intended) on issues that are specific to solo retirement, which is a topic that potentially impacts everyone. When I say everyone, I mean men and women, Boomers, mid-lifers and Millennials, and people who are retiring from professional careers or blue collar jobs. This book includes practical information on relevant topics and needs that should be considered and planned for. The only assumptions that I make in these pages is that you are planning to rebalance or restructure your life in some way to fulfill specific needs or wants, and that you need a plan to make it happen.

Many of us, especially if we are women, will likely spend a large portion of our retirement years on our own. Death or divorce is always difficult, but it can be especially devastating when it comes in retirement (and for both men and women). Everyone should plan for their future income, health, housing and social needs as if they expect to be solo at some point in the future. It's only prudent. Plan like a solo person to help ensure that you remain independent in the future. It is almost certain that you will become solo at some point.

That's another way that retirement is changing: In the coming years, solo retirees will outnumber couples in which one or more of the spouses is retired. You could say that solo retirement *is* the 'new retirement'. Now let's talk about how to plan for it.

Concerns About Retiring Solo

I've talked with and surveyed individuals who are thinking about solo retirement to ask them about the issues that concern them most. At the top of their lists: money, work, housing, community, health, lifestyle and legacy. These are topics that everyone can relate to, but they have special significance for solos.

Hands down, money is the number-one concern for just about anyone who is thinking about retirement. The big question? "Will I run out of money before I run out of years?" No one wants to outlive their resources. If you're healthy and active, you could potentially be looking at three decades of retirement or semi-retirement, with no guarantee of how far your funds will stretch.

We wonder whether the money we have will accommodate traveling and living the way that we've envisioned that we would in retirement. We worry about whether there will be enough money to carry us through if we become ill or need extended care or assisted living at some point and, if so, where that money will come from. These are potentially life-changing events and issues that everyone should be thinking about and planning for.

Retirement may also prove to be costlier than we planned for. Respondents to the *2016 Retirement Confidence Survey* reported that they had underestimated the costs of food, taxes and healthcare. Thirty-eight percent said that expenses in the early years of retirement proved to be higher than they'd expected.

Money can be an even bigger issue for solos – during both the saving and the spending years. Pensions and other financial safety nets are non-existent for most working adults. According to the Employee Benefit Research Institute, only 14 percent of American workers have a traditional pension, which is down from 38 percent in 1979. Solos also lack the financial support or 'backup' system that marriage can provide. There is no spouse to help contribute to retirement savings, bring home a second paycheck or receive a second Social Security check in the mail. Retirement savings and budgets must be built from and based on a single income, which must also cover the full share of all household expenses. In a solo household, there is usually very little room for error or for savings.

Solos aren't in a position to inherit assets or a pension like a spouse or a legal partner might, or claim survivor benefits from Social Security. The Social Security decisions that they make are critical to their financial future. There is no option to delay filing a retirement claim by opting to instead collect benefits against a retired spouse's account. (Though this may be possible if you are divorced and you were married to your ex for at least 10 years. See www.ssa.gov for details). Solos face other 'penalties' or limitations. Married couples are able to take advantage of a spousal benefit which can be worth up to 50 percent of the other spouse's benefit. Here's an example: If one spouse's benefit is worth $2,000 and the other's is only worth $500, the second spouse can switch to a spousal benefit worth $1000 – producing another $500 in income per month! Solos do not have this ability to 'pad' their monthly benefit. This is just one example of the many unfair ways that we tax or otherwise deny benefits to solo citizens in the U.S.

It's also harder for solos to sock money away in the first place. Housing takes up a much larger percentage of a solo person's monthly expenses because there is often no one to share the costs with. Ditto with home repairs, insurance and most day-to-day living expenses.

There are fewer income tax deductions to take advantage of and health insurance premiums are often higher. No wonder solos worry so much about retirement. The cost of solo living is high and saving money can be very challenging.

Work becomes another issue for 'threshold' adults who wonder whether they will be able to afford to retire in the first place. They may be thinking about new ways that they could make their old work more rewarding, or find new ways to create a paycheck out of their years of experience. Older adults, solo or otherwise, may wonder where they can get a new, potentially part-time job (preferably with benefits) and whether anyone will hire an older worker in the first place. This is a major emerging issue for solos in one-income households who need to keep at least a part-time paycheck coming in during 'retirement'.

Housing is another issue that is evolving with the Baby Boomer market. Developers are starting to pay attention as solos consider new ways to live as they grow older and we are beginning to see an increase in walkable, socially-driven communities featuring homes with smaller footprints and more shared amenities. Choices remain few, however, and there is a lot of unfulfilled demand in this sector. Developers would be smart to better capitalize on these emerging market needs. Maintaining their independence and having a nice place to live with like-minded people nearby is important to both solos and to Baby Boomers in general.

Creating a sense of community becomes increasingly important as we grow older. Humans are social animals and solos are no exception. They like to know that people are within reach, and to feel as if they are part of an extended community that provides opportunities for friendship, support, and advice or assistance when needed.

Health is a concern that starts raising its head well before retirement rolls around. Mid-life is often the time when a medical scare or the first noticeable signs of ageing provide a 'wake-up call' that encourages us to become more proactive about our health. Questions arise, including: Will I stay healthy as I get older? Who will take care of me if I get sick? What is there is no one to take care of me when I get sick? Can I afford to get sick? Do I need long-term care insurance? What does it cost? Can I afford it? It quickly becomes clear that the best strategy will be to get – and stay – as healthy as possible, starting as soon as possible. This is when many people begin to 'remodel' their lifestyle and their eating habits. Fear has always been a great motivator.

Retirement represents a huge lifestyle change for most people. For some there may be a surplus of time to work with. Others may worry about whether they will have enough time to do everything that they've been putting off until retirement finally rolled around. Still others have no idea where to begin or what to do first. Conventional retirement planning usually focuses on financial issues: how to save, invest, budget and, later, spend. Only recently have people began to really think about how they will spend their time. There is a growing number of books that promise to help you visualize your 'ideal retirement' and develop strategies to fill, use or ration your time accordingly. We'll touch on those topics in a later chapter, but from a solo planning perspective.

Some people don't want to go it alone and are in search of someone to share their retirement years. There are many different ways these days to meet a potential partner, both online and off. Follow your heart, but be cautious. Partnering up after you have developed a plan to retire solo requires care and attention to ensure that your finances and your estate are protected, and that your final wishes regarding healthcare and end of life decisions are followed.

Who will miss me when I'm gone? That's a question that many of us may ponder. We like to know that we made a difference, that someone cares about us and that they will miss us when we pass. End of life decisions about health, funerals and estates should be made clear to friends and family and put in writing to ensure that your wishes are carried out. Solos must act as their own advocates, and then make sure that they have someone whom they trust completely to enforce their preferences.

Solo retirement isn't new. A certain percentage of people have always been retiring and living on their own. Their numbers, however, are significantly increasing. Concerns about money, work, housing, community, lifestyle and legacy are gaining more and more attention as millions of Boomers make it to age 65 and beyond each year. Some markets are already evolving to keep pace. Restaurants have become more accommodating to solo diners. The travel industry is offering a wider range of opportunities for solo travelers, increasingly without single supplements. Housing is evolving, though slowly. New ways to create community are emerging. Social media and other online tools like Meetup.com have helped solos (and others) find activity partners and create a needed sense of community. More products and services will come. Marketers know a trend when they see one, and this one is here to stay.

What's really needed is a coordinated effort to address the 'high cost of being solo'. The cost of living is stacked against singles and solos at just about every economic turn. Income tax rates are higher, deductibles are fewer, Social Security benefits are scarcer and both healthcare and insurance can cost more. No other classification or group in the U.S. is as penalized for apparently 'being different' from the perceived or preferred (and subsidized) married 'norm'. Affordable, amenity-rich solo housing options can be hard to find (and often have a premium attached to them). Singles are still penalized for not wanting to share a room with a stranger (or anyone) on vacation, whether by land or cruise ship.

Solo living has a cost, and that cost is being paid by an increasing percentage of society. Society is just beginning to address what it means to be solo throughout life and into retirement. Addressing the costs of that journey needs to be the focus of that conversation.

Laying the Groundwork:

The First Step: Give Yourself Permission to Retire Solo

Being solo and living happily and independently has always been considered somewhat of a curiosity in American society. Friends, families and co-workers tend to see singleness as a 'stage' or a status that needs to be resolved or 'fixed' in some way. Solos typically pride themselves on being independent, self-supporting, strong and self-reliant. Amazingly, those aren't always considered to be flattering adjectives, especially when applied to women. Luckily, times are changing. As solo men and women become more commonplace in society – and *at all stages of life* – they are also becoming more accepted, less worried about and, frankly, sometimes envied. There's no question that marriage and partnership remain the goal for most Americans, but there is a growing recognition that almost everyone will be solo at more than one point in their lives – and sometimes for much, if not most, of their lives. The unmarried are becoming the American majority.

How did I come to write a book about solo retirement? I had been spending a lot of time thinking about what the future would look like for me as a single person and a solo entrepreneur. (I am solo both personally and professionally.) I have been divorced since 2004 and living on my own (including without children in the house full time) since 2005. In recent years, I began to realize that I might remain solo for the rest of my life. I didn't see this as a bad thing

29

(it felt more natural than searching for another mate), but I knew that I needed a plan for the future – my future. The good news? Throughout my life I have proven over and over again that I am very independent and very capable of achieving great success on my own. I graduated early from both high school and college, earned two degrees in journalism and marketing, have worked as a corporate executive, a freelance writer, a consultant, coach and advisor. I am also a solo entrepreneur and a business owner, a role that I have held for nearly 30 years. I am the owner and principal of a small but successful marketing and public relations firm that I founded in 1988 and which I continue to earn a significant income from today.

Over the years, I have had to learn how to deal with divorce, career changes, successfully starting and then running a sole proprietorship, traveling for business alone and in groups, raising teenagers as a single mom, moving across the country to a city where I didn't know anyone, starting social and activity groups, dating, making friends, traveling solo to places that I had never been to (domestically and internationally), going to movies alone and making it through the holidays on my own with a smile on my face and a true sense of contentment. I have created a thriving business, helped manage several others and played a role in the success of hundreds of public and private sector organizations. I was the primary breadwinner in all three of my marriages, built college funds for my two children (after paying off all of my own student loans by myself), bought and sold more than a dozen houses (after personally overseeing new construction or remodeling projects for many of them) and have lived on one income – mine – throughout my entire adult life. None of this was handed to me. I had to make it happen and provide for myself and my family. So I did.

I have started and funded three retirement funds for myself (as a long-time small business owner I am responsible for my own benefits and future). The first was lost in a divorce settlement, the second was diverted to fund college funds for my children (never a good idea) and the third remains a work in progress. I know that the quality of my life, both now and in the future, depends 100 percent on me and my efforts and that the quality of my retirement – whatever shape that may take – will also be entirely up to me. I have no pension or inheritance to look forward to. No alimony. No survivor or other benefits to claim. I am not looking to get married again or to have anyone else support me in the years ahead. Planning for my future is my responsibility and I intend to succeed at this just as I have succeeded in other parts of my life. I have created a plan to make the coming years (as many as 40 of them if those online life expectancy calculators are to be trusted) the four best decades of my life. That's what I deserve and I refuse to settle for less!

If I do happen to end up in a committed relationship again at some point in the years ahead (I have also learned never to say never), I will have the assurance of knowing that a path to provide for my future has already been planned. Having a plan will allow me to always make personal or professional decisions from a position of strength and *not need*. I have worked very hard to put myself in this position. It has not been easy and there have been fits and starts, mostly due to the ups and downs of my personal life. Recently I gave myself 'permission' to retire solo and to plan for the best possible future for myself. This was the critical first step for me and it is also the necessary first step for you. Accept that you will be solo at some point in the future (whether again or still), that your future is your responsibility and your responsibility alone, and then give yourself permission to plan for that time and your needs.

This is also a compelling argument for why even those who may feel happily coupled or married at the moment should always, always, always be planning for a solo future. Everyone ends up there eventually, and divorce is only one way for that to happen. You are being smart, not disloyal, when you plan for your own future financial needs. Divorces are expensive (for women and men) and the death of a partner can be financially devastating if you have been counting on a second income to cover the bills and don't have a plan in place to replace it if it disappears. Socking money away may seem impossible, especially if you are struggling now, but you have to take charge of your own future, at least by creating a plan for it. No one else is going to do the work for you. The responsibility is solely yours. Does that sound scary? That's not such a bad thing. Fear is a good motivator. If you are scared of being alone, and sick, struggling or even broke (also known as 'bag lady' syndrome, where even successful women fear that they will end up homeless and on the streets at some point), you are likely to be motivated to do everything in your power to prevent any of those outcomes from occurring.

Bag lady syndrome, by the way, really has nothing to do with reality. Women experience it from time to time (often?), usually quite illogically, and regardless of how educated or secure they may be. The 2013 *Allianz Study of Women, Money and Power* found that 49 percent of women with household incomes of $30,000 or higher often or sometimes feared that they would lose all of their money and become homeless. A third of the respondents who had household incomes of $200,000 or more reported similar fears.

Long-time solos have been dealing with feelings like these (fear, worry) for more of their lives than their married counterparts and, because they have learned how to survive on one income, they are often far better prepared for retirement – at least with better life and management skills, if not more money. I personally have felt more empowered and *more* secure since I fully embraced being (and remaining) single. Why? Because I am now planning for my future much more aggressively. When I was married – or when I thought that I might still get remarried at some point – I didn't worry about the future as much as I should have. Being coupled provides a false sense of security that can be easily shattered. Being strong and 'financially solo' (independent) is a much more reliable strategy which will pay dividends regardless of your status.

I recognized that I was solo and strong, thanks to my life experiences. I am a solo Boomer, a solo entrepreneur (actually a serial solo entrepreneur), a solo parent, solo homeowner, solo traveler, solo consumer powered by a single source of income, a solo transplant (from Illinois to Arizona), and a solo voter, volunteer and activist. At some point, I will also become a solo retiree. That probably won't happen for quite a while, at least in the traditional sense. I am fortunate to love what I do and plan to continue to working in some fashion or form indefinitely. Right now, I am rebalancing and redefining how I want to live and work in order to make the most of the coming years. That process has already produced this book and a number of related projects, including a new home in an active adult community, a lifestyle blog, a new business venture and a renewed commitment to advising new and aspiring entrepreneurs.

Over the years, I have acquired the skills that I will need to succeed in my solo retirement. Most likely, you have too. We all begin our lives as solos and spend much of our time as young adults that way. Some will remain solo. Others will revisit solo-ness over the course of their lifetime. During the years that we spend on our own, we typically learn how to dine solo, live solo, travel solo, go to the movies or the theater alone, go to events or parties without a plus one, hike and exercise solo and celebrate the holidays on our own or as a solo among couples and groups. And if we haven't, we should. Life does not require a partner to participate. The sooner you embrace that, the happier you'll be.

We have probably also learned how to survive on one income (our own), manage a household and live successfully on our own. We've learned how to make friends and create social networks. Some of us have learned how to run a business single-handedly. Most of us have learned how to find and navigate a job or career. All of these experiences help make us resourceful, independent and strong, and prepare us to create a plan to protect our hard-earned independence in retirement.

Retiring solo is about choices. It is about choosing to plan for financial independence. It is about choosing whether to continue working past the traditional retirement age and, if so, how and for how long. It is about choosing to create a sense of community that provides the social and support network that everyone needs. It is about choosing how to spend your time and with whom. It is about choosing to protect your health or strengthen it, so that you don't have to fight to regain it in the future. It is about choosing to take care of you and your needs, both now and in the future.

Most importantly, it is about choosing to begin. Throughout our lives, each of us has the power to make choices, choices that will make our lives better or worse. Regardless of what your life is like right now, good or bad, you have the power to make choices that can improve it. Only you truly know what you want and need from life. Only you can choose if, how and when to go after those things. Only you can decide where you want to be, how you're going to get there, and who you are going to take with for the journey, if anyone. You are the only person who can determine what your real needs and goals are, how you will pursue them and whether you will stay true to them throughout your life. You are the only person who has the power to make these choices. You are the only person who has the right to pass judgment on the choices that you make.

Give yourself permission to be solo or to accept that you will likely be solo again at some point. Give yourself permission to focus on you and your needs. Many of us have spent the good part of a lifetime taking care of others and their needs. Creating a plan for your solo retirement requires you to focus on you. This is truly your time. This is one thing that is – and should be – *all about you*. You are working to assure *your* future. You are planning for *your* financial and emotional goals. Rethink retirement and what it may look like for you. Create confidence in the future. Develop a plan to ensure your independence so that you aren't forced to rely on the charity or support of others. Create a strong sense of community so that you have a social, emotional or caregiving support network when you need one. All of this will help to eliminate the fear that comes from uncertainty; the fear of not knowing what the future will bring.

None of us knows what the future holds, solo or otherwise. Planning prepares us to better deal with unexpected twists and turns that may come our way. Similarly, planning for a solo retirement will leave us prepared for the greatest array of outcomes. It is not insurance, but *assurance*. Planning creates confidence and confidence is not only empowering, but healthy. Why? Because planning makes goals not only possible, but puts them potentially within reach, and that relieves uncertainty and stress.

Creating a plan for you by you has its benefits. You can make decisions and choices based on what you want and need, without having to consult a partner or having to make compromises on how much to save or how, where to live or any other myriad of lifestyle decisions. If you are married or in a partnership, you can each create a plan that addresses your respective individual needs while also recognizing and respecting the relationship. Two solo plans can work in tandem and with synergy. At the very least, a joint retirement plan should assume that one or both of the spouses or partners will be solo again at some point (whether through death or divorce) and include contingencies for that potential development.

There are practical issues and challenges to address. The next chapter will begin to outline the elements of a holistic, forward-looking solo retirement plan.

The Second Step:
Recognize the Practical Issues

Whether you are solo or otherwise, there are a number of common stumbling blocks that come with navigating retirement. They include failing to plan, underestimating how long you will live and how many years you may spend in retirement, retiring too soon, failing to save enough money, and underestimating the true cost of being retired.

Retirement planning typically doesn't gain a sense of urgency until we are rounding the corner to mid-life. Few Millennials are focused so far into the future that they have made saving for retirement a priority. Unfortunately, the same can be said for many Baby Boomers. Many are only just starting to play catch up, and only a very small percentage feel that they are 'financially prepared' for retirement. According to the U.S. Government Accountability Office, 52 percent of all workers age 55-64 do not have any retirement funds put away (although half of those people do have a pension to rely on). Among the 48 percent who reported some retirement savings, the median amount is $104,000 for households age 55-64. That translates to a retirement income of roughly $310 per month. That isn't much.

Failing to make a financial plan for retirement can make life very stressful. Failing to plan for the emotional demands of retirement will create still other challenges. Major life changes can be emotionally draining. Deciding how to make use of a bounty of newly available free time can prove to be pretty daunting. Funding retirement is one thing; living as a retired person is another. Most people overestimate how much time leisure activities will fill and assume that they will stay busy with hobbies and new interests. Others find themselves faced with too many demands competing for their newly freed up time and attention. Visualizing how you want to use your retirement will help you make better decisions and choices about how you want to spend your time. It will also help you plan for related expenses and create an appropriate budget.

The rules and rituals of the new retirement are changing. It's not all about playing golf or gardening or traveling any more. Take time to think about what retirement will look like for you, based on your interests and your goals. Think about how you will spend your time and create a plan while you are still working. In other words: before you retire. Be ready and the transition will prove much easier when it is time to deal with it.

People are living longer and it can be easy to underestimate how many years you might actually spend in retirement. According to the National Center for Health Statistics, the life expectancy of a 65-year-old has grown by 37 percent since 1950. I took three online tests and they determined that, at age 57, I likely have another 30 to 40 years ahead of me. Given that prognosis, it would not make sense for me to retire at 65 or potentially even at 70, and especially if I am still active and in good health. Delaying retirement and continuing to work at least part-time will significantly add to my nest egg, while also keeping me mentally sharp and engaged. I see it as a win-win.

The new trend among Baby Boomers is 'engaged ageing', where we remain active, involved and contributing something to society through our work, philanthropy or the creative and intellectual arts. Baby Boomers have always been notorious for measuring themselves by their accomplishments and contributions (and often also by their acquisitions). Ageing – and retirement – will be no different.

For this reason, some people who leave the workforce at the traditional retirement age of 65 may find that they have retired 'too soon'. They are not ready financially or emotionally to stop working or to step back and work fewer hours in a different setting. Work and 'going to work' provide an important sense of social belonging and emotional fulfillment that may not be fully appreciated until it is missed. Being part of an organization and a team also provides a sense of community. Abraham Maslow's Hierarchy of Needs (1943, *A Theory of Human Motivation*), charted a sense of 'belongingness' (Social/Belonging) as the first developmental step beyond the fulfillment of the Physiological and Safety needs which help to guarantee human survival. Without a sense of social belonging and community, Maslow wrote, a human could not transcend him or herself to create a sense of esteem and, ultimately, self-actualization.

In other words, work is an important part of who we are. That's another reason why a gradual or phased retirement makes sense for many people. With a phased-in retirement strategy, there is no radical change in identity or lifestyle. That's a key point to keep in mind: Retirement has become more of a process than a single event with a definite start date. Retirement is no longer about hard endings (work) and new beginnings (no longer working), which create difficult life transitions. This is likely why some people retire at a traditional age (or even earlier) and then end up going back to work again – sometimes several times. They are not ready, either financially or emotionally, to retire or they were unable to find a substitute sense of community (social or otherwise) that gave them the same satisfaction as they gained through working or going to work.

It may be that some of these people just needed a long vacation or a sabbatical to step back, relax and 'take stock' of where they are and what they want to do or be in the future. Such a 'break' could be enough to give them a 'second wind' that will keep them working, happily and in some capacity, years longer. People who have such an option will find that both they and their retirement funds can benefit from such a strategy. There is a lot to be said for taking a 'gap year' to test the waters and see if retirement is really the right strategy, or if rebalancing would work just as well.

Failing to save enough money to live comfortably on is another common mistake – and the one that people tend to worry about the most. Depending on how you choose to live in retirement (and what new interests or hobbies you plan to pursue), you may need to replace as much as 80 percent of your pre-retirement income. One source offers this quick formula: Take your current income after taxes and multiply it by 20 and then divide it by 30 years. Somewhere in that range is a broad stroke number that you can begin to work with. It will become clear very quickly that Social Security will cover only a fraction of the amount that many people need. The rest will have to come from savings, investments or a new source of working income, such as a part-time job or a new business venture.

It can be easy to underestimate the costs of retirement. Work-related expenses may be reduced or entirely gone, but finding ways to make good use of abundant leisure time can come with some pretty steep costs of its own – and especially if plans call for travel, expensive new hobbies or home remodeling projects.

Life expectancy also factors into this. On the average, women life longer than men – especially educated women. These days, women are outliving their spouses by decades and not just years. It is becoming commonplace for women to spend up to a third of their adult lives living on their own through a combination of choice, divorce or the death of a partner.

A longer life usually means funding a longer retirement and more years of managing withdrawals and expenses. At the same time, women tend to earn less money than men throughout their careers. (Financial planners call this a 'wage penalty'.) Many women have also been in the workplace for fewer years. Both factors can reduce the amount of a woman's monthly Social Security benefits and make budgeting even more important.

Funding a comfortable retirement is not an impossible goal, but it does take planning – advance planning. Building a retirement fund is a factor of time, systematic saving and compound interest or stock appreciation. The key is to know where you need to be – and approximately by when – and then create a plan to get there. The earlier you begin, the better. The later you begin, the harder you will have to work and the more you will have to save. Those are the only two options: start early or play catch up. Inertia (doing nothing) won't get you anywhere.

The appendix includes an example of categories to consider in a retirement budget. You can also find any number of examples online. I have included the framework for my personal 'un-retirement' budget, as well as the outline that helped me think my plan through. That process led to the development of my personal strategy and this book. It might also work for you.

Begin by documenting your assets, including your home, any savings or investments, expected pensions or insurance. (There is an example in the appendix.) This will give you an overview of where you are today. It is also the first step in good estate planning. Send a copy of your asset inventory to your executor or to a trusted family member. It will be an essential starting point should something happen to you. This is especially important if you are solo as you read this. There needs to be a paper or electronic trail showing what you own or have and where it can be found so that whomever is responsible for handling your estate knows where to look for your assets. Update the list annually. This is the only way to ensure that all of your money or other assets will be allocated as you wish them to be upon your death, and not end up unclaimed or lost.

Then create an income plan. Calculate your fixed expenses – things like housing, utilities, taxes, vehicle expenses, insurance, healthcare and basic grocery, sundry and clothing budgets. Add discretionary items such as travel, entertainment, gifts, charitable donations, health and beauty and other items. Your minimal goal should be to generate enough income through Social Security, savings or post-retirement work to cover your fixed and basic discretionary costs. If you've never had to create a budget – and I hadn't really gone through the exercise until I was planning for my own un-retirement – it can be a real eye-opener to see how much money goes to discretionary items each month. If your outlined expenses far exceed your expected income – and you are not willing to continue working to supplement that income – than this will be the most obvious area to 'trim the fat'. In any event, your income plan is a good starting point for your post-retirement budget. The appendix will provide more guidelines.

There are key dates and timeframes to keep in mind. Workers who are 50 or older are eligible to make catch-up contributions to 401(k) and IRA accounts each year – as much as $24,000 in 401(k) plans and $6,500 in IRAs (as of the 2016 tax year). Once workers hit 59.5 years of age there is no longer a 10 percent early withdrawal penalty on 401(k) and IRA distributions.

Regular distributions from traditional IRAs, 401(k)s and Roth 401(k)s are required beginning at age 70.5. There are some exceptions for people who are still working but don't own five percent or more of the company that they work for. Check www.irs.gov regularly to stay abreast of current tax regulations regarding retirement and retirement income.

The seven-month initial enrollment period for Medicare begins three months before your 65th birthday. If you miss the filing deadline, your premiums for Medicare Part B and D could permanently increase and you could be denied the opportunity to purchase supplemental coverage. Don't miss this deadline. If you are still working at 65 and have healthcare benefits, you need to sign up for Medicare within eight months of leaving your job or group health program to avoid the higher premiums.

You can begin claiming Social Security benefits beginning at age 62, but your benefits will be permanently reduced if you do so. The key is to know your full retirement age. If you were born between 1943 and 1954, your full retirement age is 66. If you start collecting Social Security at 62, your benefits will be reduced by 25 percent. For those born in 1960 or later, full retirement age is 67. Individuals in this group who claim benefits at 62 will receive checks that are 30 percent smaller than if they waited until full retirement age. People born between 1955 and 1959 have full retirement ages that go up by two months each year (and range between 66 and 67 years of age). The reduction for claiming early, at age 62, will range from 25 to 30 percent for this group, depending on the year in which they were born. The only way to collect 100 percent of your benefits is to wait until your full retirement age. Check www.ssa.gov for details and current guidelines and requirements.

Up until age 70, Social Security payments further increase (beyond 100 percent) by about 8 percent per year (plus cost of living increases) for workers who delay claiming them until that time. You could earn up to 132 percent of your full retirement benefit each month if you wait until 70 to file your claim. After 70, there is no additional benefit for waiting. Clearly, there's a trade-off to consider. If you file a claim at 62 (versus 70), you will receive eight additional years of payments, even though they will be 25 to 30 percent smaller each month. It can take years to make up lost time (and money) from those missed payments, even with larger checks, and if you die before reaching the breakeven point, you will have left some of your benefits on the table. Live beyond the breakeven point, however (as most people are expected to do these days) and you will fare better financially in the long run. Choosing when to claim is a personal decision that only you can make, based on your individual health and circumstances. Give it a lot of thought.

Are you already collecting Social Security as you read this and wondering if you filed your claim too soon? There are two ways that you might be able to get a 'do-over'. Within the first 12 months of claiming benefits, you can withdraw your application with Social Security. You will have to pay back any benefits that you have received to date, but you will be able to refile at a later date, and at a higher monthly benefit amount. You might also be able to suspend your benefit at your full retirement age (see above) and then wait until 70 to reclaim it. You won't have to pay back the benefits that you received, and your benefit will earn delayed retirement credits of 8 percent per year. Restart at age 70 and you could get a 32 percent boost. See www.ssa.gov for current guidelines.

Retirement is no longer a destination. It has become a journey that we are all working (literally) toward. The new retirement is no longer an end to work of any kind. In many cases, it is more likely to be the start of a new phase or a new career – more of a transition and a rebalancing process than an abrupt end and beginning. Planning for this period can help to make it the most satisfying and fulfilling time of your life.

The following chapters will address practical, social and lifestyle issues and help you develop a plan to retire happy and healthy, while preserving and protecting the financial independence that you have worked so hard to create. The bonus? You'll gain a holistic, whole-life plan for the future that you can put to work to improve the quality of your life, regardless of your relationship status.

Money and Work:

Redefining and Restructuring Work

There is no right way or wrong way to retire, solo or otherwise. Baby Boomers have been pioneers throughout their lives and now they are also reinventing retirement: when it begins, how it works and what it looks like. Our parents' generation was far more likely to subscribe to a one-size-fits-all retirement plan with a single destination roadmap (stop working, start playing). Not us. We want a plan that fits our vision of who we are and how we want to live; something flexible that works for us and how we see ourselves continuing to evolve in the years ahead. This custom-fitted interpretation of the 'new retirement' fits our sense of independence and is entirely in keeping with the solo theme of this book. Whether you choose to think of it as redesigning, redefining, reinventing or rebalancing, the goals are similar: to create a retirement that is a better fit to who we are and how we want to live. It's a new way of looking at how to plan and productively spend the 'next chapter' of our lives, whether we are solo, married, partnered or somewhere in between.

According to a May 2015 study from the Bankers Life Center for a Secure Retirement entitled *New Expectations, New Rewards: Work in Retirement for Middle-Income Baby Boomers* (May 2015), middle-income Boomers view continuing employment as an integral part of the retirement experience. Nearly one-third (28 percent) of retired Boomer respondents indicated that they are currently employed or have been employed for pay during their retirement. Of those who were not working at the time of the study, nearly half (48 percent) said that they would like to work, but were unable to do so – often citing health reasons. Six out of 10 working Boomers said that they were working because they wanted to, not because they had to. The primary non-financial reasons that they cited were to stay mentally alert (18 percent), remain physically active (15 percent) or have a sense of purpose (14 percent). Half of the employed middle-income Boomers expected to work beyond age 70 or as long as their health would allow them to.

The study also included data on non-retired middle-income Boomers. Nearly two-thirds said that they plan to work in retirement, primarily because they want to. The study also found that many of these same non-retirees also had unrealistic expectations concerning their future earning power. Only two out of 10 said that they would be willing to take a pay cut. In reality, more than half (53 percent) of employed retirees reported that they were earning far less per hour in retirement than they had in their pre-retirement careers.

Work has always been a big part of my life and a big part of my identity. It has likely been the same way for you. I can't imagine a future where I am not doing something productive, or contributing to the world in a manner that leverages my talents and experience. It's hard for me to visualize spending my 60's or even my 70's without some type of work in my life, whether that be writing, consulting, mentoring or teaching. Apparently I'm not alone. The number of older workers in the U.S. is increasing each year, according to the American Association for Retired Persons (AARP). 'Older workers are going to change the workplace as profoundly as women did', according to an online AARP advisor. That's likely very true. Age is the next barrier that will be knocked down (race and gender were earlier ones), as more and more people opt-in and continue working in some form or fashion well past the traditional age of retirement (which we will continue to define as 65 for the sake of this discussion). Solo retirees are likely to lead the movement toward an older retirement age, given their greater needs for economic security and social interaction.

Growing legions of older workers will also boost the economy. The economic impact could be as much as $12 trillion over 30 years according to analysts. Social Security will likewise get a needed boost, as more people remain in or return to the workforce and subsequently delay claiming benefits.

There are a number of reasons why Americans are choosing to work longer. One of the biggest challenges of retirement is that at the same time that there is typically less money coming in, there is also more time available to spend it. A part-time job or other income (e.g. from an online business) can relieve financial pressure and help fund activities and travel. Some people may choose to continue working in order to stay mentally active and 'sharp'. Others just aren't 'done yet' and want to continue contributing or creating in the business or non-profit sector. Still others may have had retirement forced upon them, leaving them emotionally or financially unprepared. A gradual or phased retirement makes sense for any or all of these people. Work, like community, helps keep us active, involved and engaged. That's good for our mental and physical health, all the way around.

Finding a renewed sense of community becomes critical as retirement draws near because it is our work which provides so much of our day-to-day interaction and activity. This is especially important for solos, who often use their work – and their workplace – as prime sources of social support and connectedness. Maintaining that connectedness is a benefit that can be as valuable as income in retirement – and is often much harder to replace.

Enter a whole new definition of what it means to retire – or 'un-retire', as author Chris Farrell calls it. Today's older workers have a broader range of options to consider, including part-time work that helps supplement Social Security or even delay it, so that the benefits are ultimately bigger; encore careers or businesses that capitalize on an unfulfilled passion or long-simmering business idea; and finding new ways to continue doing the work that you love with more flexibility. Not all of these options will be available to everyone or, as Farrell wrote in his book *Unretirement: How Baby Boomers Are Changing the Way We Think About Work, Community and the Good Life,* "Occupation, work history, income and education over the course of a lifetime are critical factors when evaluating prospects for un-retirement." In short, our backgrounds and work history will play a big role in how we choose to plan our future work, and also in how realistic those plans may prove to be.

The recession proved that it can be quite difficult for older workers to find new full or part-time jobs on short notice. Creating a flexible plan is key to successfully finding new work that fits your changing goals, or to redefining an existing job to make it better fit your changing lifestyle. The plan that we create is usually influenced by our careers and work lives, our health, our education and even our relationship status. The good news? With 20 to 30 years of life expectancy ahead, retirement planning could be a good time to reinvent what work means by going back to school, choosing a new career or starting a new business. History isn't necessarily destiny, nor should it be. You can re-career at any age to finally pursue a passion, become your own boss or try something new on for size.

As in many other areas, solos may have more flexibility in developing a plan and in contemplating reinvention. Although we are typically dependent on a single income – our own – we also have unilateral decision-making authority. Choices and decisions are ours to make and they can be based on our personal needs, passions and preferences.

The key is to begin – to begin visualizing, to begin planning, and to begin taking action to realize your goals. We may not know what we want to do or how long we will choose (or need) to work. We may still need to determine how much money we need to earn, how we are willing to earn that income, and what realistic options exist to implement the plan that we create. If we want or need to continue working, for whatever reason, we must chart a course to make sure that the work that we choose to do moves us forward, toward our objectives. State your goals. Write them down. They are the basis of your plan. Keep in mind that goals and needs can evolve and change as time goes by. New ideas, new opportunities and new people will always present themselves and your plan must be flexible enough to adapt to changes in how you choose to allocate your time and attention.

Also: Retirement is not irreversible. You can 'un-retire' at any time. You can go back to work. You can find a new way to work. You can create new ways to earn income, in person or online. Retirement isn't a one-way ticket anymore. We can move back and forth between retirement and un-retirement if we want to, even multiple times. That's good for us (health, wealth and social benefits) and that's good for the economy (job creation, consumer spending and, often, innovation).

Older workers have a great deal of human capital to share with the world. They bring a lot to the table in terms of knowledge, and in both work and life experience. This doesn't mean that it will be easy for an older worker to find an ideal part-time job that capitalizes on his or her experience or feeds a personal passion. One factor working in favor of Baby Boomers: the generation immediately behind us is smaller in number. There aren't enough workers coming up through the ranks to fill the jobs formerly held by Boomers who are now leaving the workforce. Granted, technological change and continued evolution in the job market have consolidated or made many of the jobs that our generation held obsolete. That same evolution, however, is also likely to open up new options and new ways to work that are less age relevant, less physically demanding and more experience or expertise-based – two areas where older workers excel.

Physical location has also become less of a factor. There is a wealth of opportunities to work at home or remotely from just about anywhere in the world, and while living abroad or travelling. As much as 43 percent of today's workforce works remotely at least part-time. The barriers to starting a business or selling a product online have also never been easier to overcome. You can become your own boss at any age, and from any corner of the world. Choose any of these strategies and you'll be right on trend. The Center for a Secure Retirement's *New Expectations* study also found that for middle-income Boomers, retirement has become a time of increased flexibility when it comes to employment. Nearly nine out of 10 (88 percent) employed Boomer retirees have work arrangements which include part-time (59 percent), freelance (18 percent) and seasonal (seven percent). Forty-two percent reported that they had become self-employed or small business owners.

It all begins with a plan, and the best place to begin is by redefining what you want work to look and feel like, and what it needs to accomplish or add to your life. For most retirees, the goal is not to replace their former income entirely, but to supplement or delay Social Security payments and/or refrain from accessing retirement savings as long as possible. Earning even just half of your former income will help considerably.

Working is an exchange of personal time for income, but it can also provide other benefits, including health insurance, and help keep living expenses manageable. Companies like Costco, FedEx, UPS and Home Depot have been pioneers in providing benefits for part-time workers. Working part-time can alternatively help pay for health insurance premiums or the cost of a supplemental Medicare policy, which then frees up funds for other interests or expenses. A part-time job also builds your social and support network – a priceless benefit. Many retirees who return to work intentionally look for jobs that will put them in touch with interesting people.

Finding meaningful work that meets our goals is all about rebalancing, restructuring, re-imagining and reinventing the traditional ways that we look at work and think about 'retirement'. There are only so many hours in the day. When we work less, we free up hours that can be used for other things. Rebalancing makes more time available for things that you want to do, learn or focus on, including passions, activities, travel, your health or your family and friends. Rebalancing sounds simple, but it can be surprisingly difficult to transition from a five-day work week with two days of weekend to seven days of a cleared schedule and open opportunity. For many new retirees, navigating the sheer 'emptiness' of the former work week calendar can be the biggest hurdle to overcome. People who say that they are happiest in retirement often also say that they had spent a lot of time thinking about what they wanted to do or achieve and then created a plan to make it happen *before they retired*. Decide how you would like to spend your time and in what proportions. How much time, ideally, do you want to devote to work, leisure, travel or learning? It doesn't matter what categories you choose to include. What matters is that you know what your categories are and what priority they hold for you. Rebalancing is about emphasis – determining what is important and devoting more time to it. This should be the starting point for your plan.

If you need at least a part-time paycheck, think about how you could restructure work to make it fit with your new goals. This can mean restructuring your work schedule (when you work), changing the geography (where you go to work or where you work from) or changing how you work. These days, you can work on contract, virtually (online) or remotely (off-site); share one or more jobs or flexible hours with other workers; or choose a seasonal or on-demand (freelance) work schedule. Work has become much more fluid and flexible than it used to be. Believe me, I know. I have been working from a home office for more than 28 years now. The scheduling and geographic flexibility that it provides is a huge lifestyle benefit.

This is also a good time to re-imagine what your work life could be. Here's your chance to do something that you have always loved; to create a career out of a passion; or take the expertise that you have acquired and use it to create a new business or pursuit. For some, this is the ideal time to go back to school and get the degree that they always wanted, or train to pursue an entirely new career. Keep in mind that you could have as many as 30 life years ahead of you. That's plenty of time for reinvention, education, training and working in a new career that you truly love – even if you choose to only work for half of that time. Universities and community colleges have become magnets for older students who are looking to re-career or reinvest in themselves. It is never too late to have the education or the career that you have always wanted, or to follow a road that was left unchosen earlier in life. Put all of the possibilities on the table. You are only limited by the limitations that you place on yourself. (I still have to remind myself of this from time to time.)

A survey by the MetLife Foundation and Encore.org reported that an estimated nine million Americans in the 44 to 70 age range are already engaged in second or 'encore' careers and another 31 million are interested in pursuing one. Over the next 10 years, according to the AARP article that documented the study, 25 percent of all Baby Boomers hope to start a business or non-profit, and half of those same people want to make a difference in the world while earning money.

Reinvention can also mean using your decades of experience or expertise to take on the teaching, coaching or consulting career that you have always been interested in. You can pair a Master's degree with your years of experience and teach as an adjunct at the community college level. You can put years of sales or customer service experience to work to become a trainer or online service rep. Look beyond your resume and consider the skills that you have developed, the experiences that you have had, and the types of companies that you have worked for or with. Somewhere in that skillset is the foundation for your next career or business venture. It just takes some reimagining and repurposing to see it – and then some initiative to act on it.

Enter the Encore Entrepreneur

Entrepreneurship is re-imagining, reinvention and re-careering on steroids. You are creating a company and a job for yourself and potentially also creating additional jobs for others. If there was a lesson that came out of the 2008 recession (and there were many of them), it was that each of us is ultimately responsible for assuring our own careers, compensation and retirement. Owning your own business gives you more control over these outcomes. There is more risk and more responsibility, but there is also the chance for greater control and reward.

Entrepreneurship is a viable option for people who want to keep earning an income on their terms. You are basically creating your own job and your own work. Age becomes irrelevant. If you are one of the 63 percent of Americans who plan to work during their 'retirement', small business ownership could be a good way for you to put your decades of experience to work. We accumulate a lot of expertise, skills and connections during our first careers. Entrepreneurship can leverage and put those assets to work in a new 'encore' business.

Entrepreneurship can also be very flexible. Technology has made it much easier to get a business up and running, and to manage it alone or with partners. Portable technology has also made it easier to work on the go, from anywhere in the world. Startup costs can be very low, especially in the knowledge (e.g. consulting or technology) and creative sectors. You can choose to work virtually and completely online and avoid the costs and commitments of paying for and staffing a physical 'bricks and mortar' office. You can sell and distribute products through online portals such as Amazon, eBay and Etsy – sometimes without ever touching the product or printing a shipping label. Or you can choose to create a website and become an affiliate that earns money from leading visitors to products or other sites. The options are endless. Small businesses are typically very nimble. You can react relatively quickly to changes (and opportunities) in the marketplace, technology or the economy and adjust your business strategy as needed. Larger companies cannot adapt as easily.

Entrepreneurship is an ideal encore career for someone who values independence. As an entrepreneur, you are captain of the ship. You get to steer it whichever way you see fit. You will call all of the shots and make all of the decisions. You get to decide how much to work, what markets to pursue, when to outsource, automate, pivot or pursue a new opportunity. At the same time, it's also up to you to keep the business afloat. Your success will depend largely on your personal abilities and effort. You assume all of the risk but will also reap all of the rewards. I have been running my own firm successfully for nearly 30 years now and I cannot imagine a better way to work. I can fine-tune my business model and my marketing as needed to adjust to changes in the marketplace, capitalize on new ideas or trends, or position my company to fulfill a newly identified need for our services. I am continually rebalancing to ensure that my business meets my needs as well as those of my clients. I run a 'key man' operation which means that, at the end of the day (or at the start or anytime in between), success or failure depends on me and me alone. I like that. If that's not your cup of tea, there are ways to adapt the strategy to include partners or to adopt established business models or brands, such as franchises, which can reduce risk.

Solo entrepreneurship is not for the undisciplined or the faint of heart. Yes, it is very rewarding and exciting, but it can also be scary, frustrating and exhausting. I have worked from a home office for nearly 30 years now and for many of those years I worked 50 to 60 hours a week (and even when my children were young and I was active in the community). The good news is that I was able to choose *which* hours to work (for the most part), as long as I met my commitments and deadlines. That in its own right is very freeing.

According to the MBO study, *The State of Independence in America*, there were 30.2 million independent workers over the age of 21 in the U.S. in 2015. The study defines these 'independents' as 'Americans of all ages, skills and income levels who turn to freelancing, contract work, consulting and temporary assignments or on-call work regularly each week for income, opportunity and satisfaction'. The study further reports that the independent workforce is not only broadening, but also getting younger. The number of Millennials (ages 21-35 in the MBO study) grew from 1.9 million in 2011 to 5.35 million in 2015 – an increase of nearly 300 percent.

The number of part-time independent workers is also increasing. People who regularly work independently between one and 15 hours per week numbered 12.4 million in 2015. Over the next five years, MBO expects the number of full-time and part-time independent workers in America to grow by 25.4 percent to 37.9 million in 2020 – or approximately 30 percent of the private, non-farm workforce.

The report also credits independent workers, including solopreneurs, as job creators who hired other independent workers and added more than $1.15 trillion of revenue to the economy (roughly seven percent of Gross Domestic Product, or GDP). The independent economy, according to MBO, is growing more rapidly than the U.S. economy at large. In 2015, independents spent approximately $101 billion to hire other independent workers on a contract basis, which was up nearly 10 percent from 2014. This, reports MBO, is the equivalent of employing 2.4 million full-time workers via traditional hiring.

Interestingly, the report goes on to say that by the year 2020, about half of the entire U.S. workforce will have been independent at some point in their work lives. That's very similar to the evolution of Americans' personal lives. Today, almost everyone will spend more time on their own, as a solo, than they will with a spouse or partner. Now that experience is also carrying over to our work lives. Americans are living and working more independently than ever before. The parallels can't be coincidental.

I have been a solopreneur throughout my career (and a solo for much of my life). Solopreneurs are self-employed business owners who work and run their businesses alone, without employees. (The people who work with me work are independent contractors, not employees.) Solopreneurs are often professionals or former professionals with skills or expertise to share. Thanks to technology, they can now also be store owners, publishers and consultants in any sector and serve potential customers in any part of the world. Solopreneurs have no plans to hire employees in the future (although more than one-half of all U.S. small businesses that now have employees expanded from solopreneur status) and use independent contractors to provide needed services (virtual assistants, design, accounting and technical support services). They are typically not looking to expand into multiple (or any) physical locations and are often internet-based or powered. Many solos run their businesses from a home office (like I do) and have very low overhead costs. They have complete decision-making authority, as well as responsibility for making sure that taxes get paid, paperwork gets done and that new business is found, won and successfully served.

People who make good solopreneurs tend to be disciplined workers. They are comfortable with using technology to promote themselves and their business, and to collaborate, communicate and work with others. They have a strong desire for financial and creative freedom and have the passion and the drive to fulfill their dream.

They are comfortable making decisions, setting goals and acting on opportunities. If these traits describe you, then entrepreneurship may be a good strategy to create income in your 'un-retirement' years.

And you won't be alone. Older Americans start more businesses than any other age group and it has been that way for more than a decade, according to the U.S. Small Business Administration (SBA). Between 1996 and 2013, the 55 to 64 demographic started businesses at a higher rate than those in their 20's or 30's. In 2013, in fact, nearly 25 percent of all small businesses were started by an entrepreneur who was in the 55-plus age group. "Today's entrepreneurial 60-year-old could be the 2020's entrepreneurial 70-year-old," predicts the Ewing Marion Kauffman Foundation Study of Entrepreneurship. The study report went on to forecast that the U.S. could be 'on the cusp of an entrepreneurship boom' due to the health, motivation and impressive activity levels of un-retiring workers in its largest generation.

That makes a lot of sense. In addition to starting a wealth of new businesses, Baby Boomers are also providing a wealth of new business opportunities for entrepreneurs of any age. These opportunities go far beyond healthcare and ageing-related sectors to also include products and services that are needed and wanted by Boomers who are working longer, traveling more, are more active and are also more focused on health, fitness and appearance than any generation that has come before them. It's a win-win all the way around: older entrepreneurs creating new businesses and jobs by serving the ageing Baby Boomer market. Who, after all, would know its needs and wants better than a Boomer entrepreneur?

There will also be expanded opportunities to serve the 'solo market' with products and services that fulfill the needs of people who live, work and travel on their own. Think about the products you'd like to be able to buy or the services that you'd like to be able to access as a solo (and without paying a premium). If you can devise a new or better (easier, more cost-effective, reliable or faster) way to source, access and fulfill those needs, you probably have a good business model to build on. Solo and ageing are two markets that are definitely coming together. If you are a solo Baby Boomer and you can come up with an idea that serves both markets at the same time, you likely have a winner on your hands!

There are a lot of good resources to help you think through your idea and get your business off the ground. The SBA offers an online Encore Entrepreneurship program (see the appendix) that asks questions which walk you through your concept, while also explaining what it takes to successfully start and run a small business.

The SBA's Small Business Development Center (SBDC) program offers counseling and training to new and aspiring entrepreneurs through its offices in all 50 states and each of the U.S. territories. SBDC business analysts and counselors will work with you to think through your business concept and help you develop a business plan to make it happen. Most importantly, their counselors will help you ask and answer questions that your friends and family may not bring up in their desire to encourage and applaud your efforts.

The SBA offers similar services through its SCORE (Service Corps of Retired Executives) program. SCORE advisors can connect you with a mentor, who will work with you to get your new business off the ground. Both of these SBA programs offer guidance in marketing, technology, finance, management, export and import assistance, and can provide you with access to other resources that can help guarantee a fast start. The input and advice that you receive is sure to save you time and money in the long run. SBA data also shows that small business owners who work with an SBDC or SCORE counselor have a greater likelihood of success. See the appendix for program websites.

Over my career, I have worked as an SBDC business analyst in Illinois and Arizona, and as a consultant to SBDC state networks and related programs in Alaska, Arizona, Illinois, Maryland and New Mexico. A good deal of this work included writing program reports for the SBA on the impact of SBDC programs. Those experiences provided me with a front row seat to watch the emerging success stories of small businesses across the country. Whenever someone tells me that they are thinking of starting a business, I encourage them to check out the SBA website to learn about the resources that are available to them. It's a very good place to begin.

I have also taken this experience and paired it with three decades of successful business building experience to create a new venture that is playing a featured role in my own rebalancing plan. My new business indulges my passion for working with new and aspiring business owners to help them confront the challenges of startup and growth by offering personalized one-on-one advising by phone, web or in person. The company, Encore Business Advisors, also provides website development, social media management and marketing consulting services that can help new businesses get off to a stronger start. It is a perfect example of pairing experience, expertise and passion to respond to a growing market trend (encore entrepreneurship) while meeting personal goals. You can learn more about it at www.encorebusinessadvisors.com.

Over the years, I've had the opportunity to work with and lead chambers of commerce, civic groups and professional associations, and to make presentations to a wide range of business audiences. Networking – putting yourself and your offering in front of other people – is a good way to create visibility for yourself and your new business. It's also a great way to meet contacts who can connect you with other independent service providers and small business owners. This is especially important for solopreneurs, who need to leverage visibility and word of mouth to help their solo-run businesses succeed quickly and cost-effectively.

Funding Your Solo Retirement Lifestyle

Planning for retirement is no easy task. There is money to be saved (which is hard), set aside (even harder) and then left untouched (sometimes impossible), and plans to be first made and then revisited as life inevitably changes.

Saving for retirement can be especially challenging for people who are solo during much of their working years. Solos live on one income, their own, and are usually the only person who is contributing to their retirement. Social Security, tax laws and often healthcare and insurance premiums are stacked against them. The 'singles' tax is very much alive and well in the U.S. in the form of benefits, deductions and reduced rates that are only available to married couples. These 'unmarried' penalties make it even harder for solos to save for retirement, or to live comfortably in retirement in later years.

The '10-year retirements' of yesterday are gone (where people retired at 65 and then lived to an average age of 75). People are living longer – sometimes a lot longer. Many of us could spend as many as 30 years in the new post-65 'retirement years'. This means that we have to save more money to fund more years, and we have to find ways to make the money that we do squirrel away last even longer. In an ideal situation, we will continue to earn enough income so that we can keep our hands off of our retirement savings as long as possible, and then only take the minimum distribution (currently recommended at three to four percent per year) after that.

There are five basic ways to potentially achieve your retirement goals. The first is to save as much money as possible. Obvious, perhaps, but rarely easy to do. It can be very difficult to put money away when there are bills to pay, shiny things to buy or children or other family members who need our help. Endless experts will tell you that the easiest way to sock money away is to have it automatically deducted from your paycheck and placed directly into a 401(k) or other savings plan, where it may be matched by your employer. If you are self-employed, you have the option to open a self-directed 401(k) and match your contributions with contributions from your company. It can be a good way to sock some serious money away as your business begins to get traction – but you still have to possess the personal discipline to not only start the process, but also stick to it.

It is always a good idea to seek professional advice when analyzing and planning for your personal situation. I am not a tax attorney or a financial planner. What works for me may not work as well for you. This book is designed to get you thinking about the future, encourage you to create a plan and then inspire you to start putting your plan to work. Start by outlining your goals and your preferred timelines. A reputable financial planner (recommended by someone you know who has personally worked with that advisor) can assess your personal situation, help you work out the numbers and then assist you in building a plan to make your goals a reality.

The second strategy is to continue to work as long as possible. It is, by far, the best way to build savings while also making it easier to keep your fingers out of your retirement nest egg. You may think that you're ready for retirement, but you may really just need a change of scenery, a new way to work or a new work environment. An encore career may be just the ticket to keep you working and/or producing income for several more years (or longer). The possibilities are broad and fairly endless. You could work part-time, start a business, become a coach or a consultant, open an online store and sell items on the internet, provide a much-needed service to people in your area (or beyond), write and publish books, teach or purchase income-producing properties that help create passive income. The list goes on and on. Always be on the lookout for new ways to make money or to create income of some kind. As technology, markets and society continue to evolve, there will always be a new idea or opportunity to consider, or a new need to fulfill.

Another key to saving more money: reduce your housing costs and get rid of expensive installment debt. Lower your spending levels and start living (and spending) as if you were already retired. You'll find it easier to sock away more of your income now and you will also be better prepared for the economic transition to retirement when your paycheck ends and your cash flow changes.

Make it your plan to defer claiming Social Security benefits as long as possible. The earliest age to claim regular retirement benefits is 62. Once you file your claim it is typically irrevocable. (There are some exceptions.) Do it too early and you can leave a lot of money on the table. On the average, people typically tend to begin claiming benefits between 65 and 67 years old. It pays to wait even longer. For each year that you delay benefits past 62, you could gain a six to eight percent increase in lifetime annual benefits. Deferring Social Security claims until age 70 will provide the greatest possible monthly benefit – often significantly more. Example: If you were born between 1943 and 1954 and wait until age 70 to file your claim, you will get 132% of the monthly benefit that you would have received at age 65 because you delayed getting benefits for 48 additional months. Analysts compare that to earning an eight percent return on the money that you didn't claim during those years. Try finding a return like that anywhere else in today's market! If you are in good health as you near full retirement age, waiting a little bit longer could be an economic no-brainer.

At age 70, the monthly benefit stops increasing, so there is no reason to delay your claim beyond that age. (See www.ssa.gov/mystatement for an online statement of what your benefits would be at 62, 65 and 70 years of age.)

Continuing to work to 65 and beyond makes it easier to delay claiming Social Security benefits as long as possible. You can also continue to contribute to your 401(k) or other retirement accounts at the same time. It's a win-win, all the way around as your savings grow at the same time that your future benefits increase.

The Social Security system is complex and offers a wide range of benefits that are worth investigating. If you are at least 62 years old and divorced, but were married for more than 10 years, you can collect Social Security benefits on your ex-spouse's account if you have not remarried. The amount that you can collect is based on his or her work record and does not impact his/her benefits. There are restrictions, which you can learn about on the SSA website at www.ssa.gov. If you are Suddenly Solo due to the death of a spouse, you could qualify for survivor benefits. The SSA website is the authoritative source for all questions about retirement or other Social Security benefits. Take the time to review it thoroughly and then subscribe to updates.

Successful saving also means having an emergency fund available to handle unexpected expenses. The last thing that you ever want to do is pay early withdrawal penalties on designated retirement funds because you don't have any cash available in an emergency. This is especially critical for solos, who have only themselves and their incomes to rely on. Ideally you want to have six months of living expenses in liquid assets, but three or even one is better than having nothing. Yes, a credit card can tide you over in an emergency, but you still have to repay that expense and the interest that will incur on top of the original amount. And: Your emergency fund should be even larger once your working income ends. Having cash available to work with will help avoid costly investment sales or withdrawals during times when the market is down (which locks in losses). You can pay your emergency fund back with investment funds at a later date, when the market is stronger.

Sit down and create a post-retirement budget that details your expected income from work, Social Security, the amount that you expect to withdraw from your investments and other sources, and your expected living expenses. Be realistic (and frugal – remember that you may be planning to make your money last for decades). Try 'test driving' your budget by living that way for a year. You may be surprised at how little you can get by on once your goals (and your perspective) change.

The years right before retirement are often our highest earning years. Resist the temptation to spend more during that time and choose to sock more money away instead. The Internal Revenue Service makes it easy for taxpayers who are over 50 to play 'catch up' on their retirement funds with accelerated contributions. Now is the time to put any extra income away for the future. Or as one retirement expert puts it: "I've never met anyone who complained about putting away too much money for retirement."

Also use your high-earning, most successful career years to build the professional networks, skills and other resources that you may need to re-career or otherwise earn additional income after you leave your current job. It will be much easier to lay the groundwork for your next career – or even a part-time endeavor – while you are still working full-time.

If you are thinking about relocating to a new city or buying a smaller home to retire in, experts advise that you do it *before* you stop working. It will be easier to get a mortgage – even a smaller one – while you still have a steady income. Ditto if you are planning to refinance and stay in your current home.

Given longer, healthier life spans, the best strategy for many people will be to work as long as possible. This makes it possible to continue building savings while deferring Social Security. It will also shorten the total number of years that you will need to live off of your retirement money. With many of us looking at up to three decades of active living (and spending) beyond the former benchmark of 65, that could be the most compelling argument of all.

Housing:

Rethinking a Roof Over Your Head

A few years ago, I began thinking about how I would choose to live if I could live any way that I wanted to. The plan that evolved in my head (and since then, on paper) include a small age-restricted 'village' of eight to 12 cozy villas – really single unit, single-level townhouses – that are arranged in a rambling circle, with backyards facing in and driveways facing out, around a large common area and a community building. The common area would include a pool and hot tub, gardens and walkways that meandered between the homes and the common assets.

The community building would be just large enough to have a central 'gathering room', a kitchen and a few smaller rooms where a visiting masseuse, hair stylist, manicurist or other service provider could 'set up shop' and work with interested residents one day each week on a regular schedule. I envisioned shared dinners and happy hours, group workout sessions with a visiting trainer and opportunities for residents to learn from each other. The community building, pool and grounds would be maintained by workers paid for through monthly assessments. Residents would pay for other personal services, as needed and used.

I've left one important detail out. I always envisioned this idyllic little community – and that's exactly what it would be, a community – as being populated only by women. The residents would all be older (50+) women living in their own homes in their own private spaces, but with the ability to open their back doors at any time and step off of their patios and out into a social and community support system that would wrap itself around them like a warm hug. These would be women that I would live near, but not with, and with whom I would laugh, cry, learn, work and (hopefully) grow old with. They would watch out for me and I would watch out for them. If one of us failed to show her face at some point during the day, on any given day, someone would come looking for her by evening, or at least call to make sure that all was well. The real beauty of it all was that, at the end of the day or whenever and as often as I chose, I could go into my home, close my door and enjoy my space and privacy, just as I do now. It really would be the best of both worlds: community and castle; social and solo.

I wasn't sure how to get around fair housing laws, which prohibit discrimination based on gender, or ensure that when a property changed hands it would transfer to someone who shared the same community goals. Eventually I realized that gender wasn't really an issue. What was most important was that everyone who lived in this very small, very close knit development was passionate about both finding and providing a true sense of shared community with their neighbors.

I even came up with a name for it: *Entourage*. By definition, the word means 'a group of people attending or surrounding an important person'. Each of us would be that important person. Each of us would surround and watch out for each other while living on our own.

I searched the internet high and low looking for a community like this, or a developer who offered anything that even remotely resembled this concept. Along the way, I learned a lot about co-housing, pocket neighborhoods and other ways to live in community (which we will talk about shortly), but I couldn't find exactly what

I was looking for. To this day I have been unable to find a housing product that even comes close.

This is interesting to me as a marketing expert, because just about every woman (solo or otherwise) whom I mention this idea to gets very excited by the possibilities. They can visualize what living in a community like that would be like, and they want in – *now*. Solos are especially intrigued by the concept. I know, without hesitation, that a housing product like this – smaller-scale, community-oriented housing which offers privacy, community spaces and shared amenities – would be an instant hit with solo women and men in their 40's, 50's and beyond who are active, social, working or retired, and in search of a sense of community. I also know that it's the concept and the way that it is executed that is important, not the shape or form of the house itself. The product could be free-standing homes, townhomes, condos or apartments. The key, as in many things, would be in the marketing: targeting people – in this case active, solo adults – who share a common interest in 'living together while also living alone'.

My research also led me to discover Bella DePaulo, PhD, a social psychologist based in Santa Barbara, California who has written a number of very good books on what she calls 'singlism' or, as the subtitle to her 2006 book '*Singled Out*' reads: '*How singles are stereotyped, stigmatized and ignored, and still live happily ever after*'. DePaulo was the first author to really shine the spotlight on what it's like to be single in America, and she hasn't stopped doing research or writing about the topic since.

In her 2015 book, '*How We Live Now*' – which builds on the topic of singles and singlism to look at alternative styles of living for solos and other 'non-traditional' households – DePaulo calls the simultaneous search for interdependence, community and independence a mission to find 'the right mix of sociability and solitude'. "When I ask people what matters to them in deciding how and with whom to live," she wrote, "they mention everything from dealing with the tasks of everyday life to existential concerns about who will care for them later in life. On a psychological level, there are two things that just about everyone wants, though in vastly different proportions. They want time with other people and time to themselves."

In preparation for the book, DePaulo interviewed dozens of people whom she calls 'life space pioneers' – people who are 'creating new ways to live and love' by writing their own scripts. The books' chapters cover a rainbow of new (or newly embraced) ways to create homes, families and housing styles that are gaining traction across the U.S. (sometimes after being conceived or popularized overseas). Among them: multi-generational and horizontal family living, living with friends or housemates, living in community (which includes co-housing and is the category where my housing vision would fit most closely), new 'couples', and 'life spaces' for the new old age (including senior co-housing, villages, active adult communities and living solo). Each is an example of the many non-nuclear ways that people – and especially solos – are choosing to creatively live alone, together, or alone while together.

It is a common misconception that people who live alone are unhappy or lonely. Nothing could be further from the truth. According to DePaulo: "Living alone and being alone are hardly the same, yet the two are routinely conflated. In fact, there's little evidence that the rise of living alone is responsible for making us lonely. Research shows that it's the quality, not the quantity of social interactions that best predicts loneliness. What matters is not whether we live alone, but whether we *feel* alone. As divorced or separate people often say, there's nothing lonelier than living with the wrong person."

I can testify to that from my own experience. You're likely to agree if you've ever lived with someone – whether a spouse, a partner, a friend or a roommate – whom you didn't get along with very well. Being confined to a space – no matter how large – with someone who is a bad match can feel far more isolating than being in that same space by yourself ever could. I have lived in small apartments and huge houses with people who were unhappy and difficult to be around. Each experience was equally stifling. There is an old saying: 'It is better to be alone than in bad company.' Nothing could be truer.

Living with other people also carries a cost that many people are not willing to bear, e.g. lack of privacy, required compromise, unavoidable friction, shared decision making, differing personal habits, friends or design taste. The list goes on and on. When you live solo, you truly are the king or queen of your own castle.

Living alone makes it possible to do what you want, when you want to and on your own terms. This is often very liberating for women who find themselves freed from taking care of a family and a family home, sometimes for the first time.

Many people will live on their own as solos more than once, as they move through different life stages and relationship experiences. Each time, they bring a new perspective to the arrangement. Solo living definitely holds a strong appeal for many. For some people, living solo is a choice that is made early and then embraced for life. For others, living solo becomes a welcome new habit. The longer we live on our own, the more difficult it can become to imagine a life lived otherwise. The real secret of solo living is that it's better than anyone imagines. It's also more expensive, but most solos will tell you that the freedom and flexibility is definitely worth the cost.

What matters is not that we live alone, but whether we feel alone, according to Eric Klinenberg, the author of the 2012 book *Going Solo, The Extraordinary Rise and Surprising Appeal of Living Alone*. The two are hardly the same, he wrote, citing evidence that suggests that people who live alone compensate by becoming more socially active, regardless of their age. DePaulo's research also bore that out, reporting that married couples tend to become more insular and 'inner-focused' (which can lead to feelings of isolation that rarely get talked about), while singles are typically more outgoing and active in their communities.

Most Baby Boomers still retire as part of a couple and their numbers are having the greatest influence on the housing market. The share of households headed by someone who is at least 55 years old will grow every year through 2019, when that category will account for nearly 45 percent of all U.S. households, according to the National Association of Home Builders. That's a huge market.

One in every eight U.S. residents is now 65 or older according to AARP, and the vast majority of the group – nearly 90 percent – say that they want to age in place (remain in their current home). That is creating a big market for features that help to make homes more 'senior friendly'. Ageing in place can also mean downsizing to a smaller home, condo or townhome in the same community, which preserves an existing social network while making expenses and day-to-day life more manageable.

My gut tells me that younger Boomers and the generation that will follow them are more interested in 'ageing in community' than ageing in place, and that they are also more willing to relocate to find what they want (along with friendlier taxes). There is some data to support that, according to AARP, which reports that their members who are younger than 65 are far more likely to move in a given year (13%) than those who are 65 or older (4%). These people will move for a variety of reasons, with downsizing and retirement among them. A move may also be in response to a change in status, a family member's need, a change in health or a desire for a change of scenery. The 'new retirement' is becoming more mobile than ever.

Active adults who are still working, semi-retired or in the earliest years of retirement are more attracted to areas that are vibrant, walkable, multi-generational and often urban, and to housing that provides a physical and spiritual sense of community. We are falling back in love with the idea of having neighbors again.

DePaulo sees a similar trend in *'How We Live Now'* when she writes that "Friendships have emerged as the essential twenty-first century relationship." People want to avoid isolation, create community, and create resource and support networks while also ideally reducing their housing costs and responsibilities. "The best places to live are also the best places to retire, with connections to others, choice, mobility, security and stability," she wrote. Money is a factor, as it always is, but it does not have to be a disqualifier. Creativity can help compensate for a lack of cash.

In a 2016 follow up article in the online publication, *Nautilus*, DePaulo drilled down to the real driver behind today's housing evolution: choices. "What is so different about the way we're living now is that we have more options than ever before to choose the life we want," she wrote. "Of course we are constrained by whatever resources and money we have, but I found in writing my book, *How We Life Now*, that even people who were very constrained in their finances could still find a very satisfying life to live."

The communities that most often make the 'best places to retire' lists these days tend to be less about good weather and more about offering attainable housing, active living, plentiful recreational opportunities, lower taxes and vibrant economies that can support businesses and jobs. Or as Paul Irving, chairman of the Milken Institute Center for the Future of Ageing, put it: "Successful ageing is about more than just snow." Another stereotype knocked down.

In *How We Live Now*, DePaulo reports how she asked each of her interviewees to answer these three questions: "Of all the different ways you have lived, what felt like the best fit for you? What was the happiest time in your life? How would you live if you could magically live any way at all? Pretend that money is no object, and neither is anything else." I had my response already visualized before I read that section of her book. I had asked myself many of the same questions during the process that produced both the 'Entourage' idea, my 'unretirement plan' and this book. Now it's your turn. Think about your life and your situation and what is important to you. Consider your finances and whether you will need or want to continue to earn an income. Where will your support network come from? How social are you? How much privacy do you need? How would you choose to live if you could live any way that you wanted to? You may find the beginning of your answer in DePaulo's book and in the following section on new ways to live in community.

New Ways to Live in Community

According to an AARP Foundation, the U.S. will face a critical shortage of affordable housing for its 50-plus population in the coming years. The study, which was done in cooperation with Harvard University, reports that group will swell to more than 133 million people by 2030 (up 70 percent since 2000 alone).

The increase in solo households began earlier and is even more profound worldwide, according to social psychologist Bella DePaulo, who cited a Euromonitor International study reporting that the number of one-person households more than doubled between 1980 and 2011 – from about 118 million to 277 million. That number is expected to climb to 334 million solo households by 2020. "Individuals, not couples or clans or other social groups, are fast becoming the fundamental units of society," DePaulo wrote in a March 2016 *Nautilus* blog article.

The U.S. solo market for housing, goods and services is also huge and growing. A 2014 Census Bureau report documented that more than 107 million Americans age 18 and older were unmarried and that in excess of 33 million individuals lived alone (more than a quarter of all U.S. households). The census study further reported that the percentage of one-person households (solos) had grown by 10 percentage points between 1970 and 2012, an increase of 17 to 27 percent of the total population. Single-person households were the fastest growing household type in the last census count. The data (updated since) does not provide any indication that this trend is going to reverse any time soon.

Some of that has to do with the ageing of America. As Eric Klinenberg reported in *Going Solo*, fewer older people are remarrying after the death of a spouse – only two percent of widows and 20 percent of widowers ages 65 and older remarry in the U.S. Part of that has to do with the availability of partners, but friendship may be the better indicator of remarriage, according to Rutgers University sociologist Deborah Carr, who found that elderly men who have a lot of friends become as unlikely to remarry as women.

The rising solo tide is changing the way that we live, and the way that we want to live. No doubt, DePaulo's 2015 book *The Way We Live Now* is the best study of evolving housing options in America. It is a must-read for anyone who is searching for new ways to live solo or in community. There are a lot of good ideas being tested, and proven, but there isn't a lot of inventory – yet. As a marketing person, I watch evolving markets to spot emerging product and service needs. I study demographic trends to identify business opportunities. I look at technological innovation and see new ways to communicate, work, learn, sell and live.

Housing developers are very much marketing people, but they also tend to be careful investors – and anyone who has tried to sell a home in a declining real estate market can't blame them for being cautious. Real estate development is risky and expensive, but it is also potentially very profitable. The trick is to be able to spot long-term demographic trends (not style trends) and be ready to capitalize on them. That requires perfect timing, and being just a little bit ahead of the curve. That's where the risk comes in.

Senior housing is a multi-billion-dollar industry. Developers don't like to invest in unproven models (e.g. my Entourage villa concept) but once they do (more likely, once they see a more adventurous developer successfully test the market), they will realize that there is a lot of pent up demand. A growing number of people are in search of smaller-sized housing that is livable, efficient and attractive, and they want it to be close to activities, services and other vibrant, interesting people.

New-style housing developments that are built and marketed to appeal to solos, active retirees and urban professionals tend to sell or rent out very quickly. The redevelopment of Denver's former Stapleton airport into a mixed used development featuring multi-generational housing options and dedicated senior residences, is a good example. Aptly named Stapleton, it is considered a national model for urban development. Downtown Denver is a hot-bed of redevelopment projects featuring new ways to live. Among them: A project that is converting a former hotel into micro-apartments, where more than a third of the units are only 330 square feet in size and most of the balance (more than 300) offer only 665 square feet of living space. The apartments are targeted at Denver's growing tech and professional populations, many of whom are Millennials. They are also ideal for solos who want to live within reach of everything that the city has to offer. The city's new light rail system has opened the urban core up to a wide range of lifestyles and ages.

Housing and housing-related product marketers are waking up to emerging opportunities in the solo housing market beyond Denver. The market is starting to produce new offerings of smaller-sized units located in walkable, often urban or semi-urban areas which offer easy access to shops, restaurants and entertainment. Free-standing homes as small as 1,000 square feet are also becoming easier to find, which is saying a lot for an industry that has primarily focused on designing homes for large families. Even the term 'single-family housing' is being replaced with 'free-standing homes' as solo homebuyers – and especially female solo homebuyers – become a growing presence in developer sales offices. As author Rebecca Traister noted in her 2016 book *All the Single Ladies*, "Single female life is not a prescription, but its opposite: liberation." That liberation increasingly includes single women buying and living alone in their own homes.

It also includes women picking up and retiring to a foreign country. Solo women especially are seeking out 'ex-pat' communities around the world. Anthropologist Liesl Gambold looked at that growing trend in 2013 and found that it is easier for women, who tend to be very good at creating social connections and support networks, to make the transition to living in a foreign country then men – especially if they are making the move alone. Cost of living was a big factor for most singles who chose to move to another country. It remains very (and most) expensive to live alone in the U.S., Canada and England.

Still other ageing Boomers want to stay close to home in retirement to preserve family, work and social connections. Ageing in place has become a big industry in the U.S. A myriad of businesses have sprung up to help Baby Boomers retrofit their homes to make them more user-friendly as they age. Many of the features that they are adding – including rocker light switches, lever door handles, grab bars, adjusted counter heights, side-by-side fridges and ovens, and color-contrasted stairs – are also being offered as options in new home developments, and particularly in 'active adult' communities, which are evolving and being marketed to appeal to today's younger, healthier and far more active residents.

Ageing in place and active adult living have one clear thing in common: They are both housing strategies which seek to maintain or build a sense of community, a circle of friends and a support network. Americans may not mind getting older as much as they used to, but they are still concerned about ageing alone or in isolation. The housing industry is slowly evolving to respond to this growing need.

Community is the continuity that we all seek in an ever-changing world. Social circles and support networks can survive death or divorce, can have many different facets (different friends for different interests and activities) and can change and evolve as we do. We may not want to be involved or participate in the community

– whatever form it may take – every minute of every day, but we do like to know that it's there and available when we need it or want it. As solos, we may like and even prefer to live alone, but we want to be able to do so in an environment which also provides us with social connections, opportunities for activities and the sense of community that we crave. Community makes it easier to live alone by making it possible to 'live alone near others' (the core of my Entourage concept). The ability to do so is very appealing to solos of all ages. This is the market that housing developers need to actively cater to and capture.

There are many new (and not so new) ways to live that can provide a sense of shared community. Among them: Neo-traditional communities (also known as 'smart growth' or 'new urbanism') which cluster free-standing cottage or town homes around common areas with shared walkways in pocket neighborhoods; age-targeted apartment or condo complexes that offer shared spaces and on-site amenities; co-housing communities that are similar to neo-traditional developments, but typically have residents share administration, upkeep and chores (more communal style living); senior intentional co-housing communities where residents age in their own homes, but close to others; active adult communities which are amenity-laden and typically built in outlying areas, making them activity rich but often less walkable; and the new wave of 'senior' housing options, which include independent, assisted and transitional living – often housed within the same building or complex.

Shared housing is also becoming visibly more popular, as DePaulo and others have pointed out. It is also evolving far beyond the typical roommate model. Solos who find themselves with over-sized homes to share are opening their homes to one or more roommates who come to live together under one roof, often in their own suites or even floors. Groups like the Golden Girls Network and Women Living in Community help connect potential housemates with each other. Another option is for an individual or a group of potential co-owners to buy or build a home that has one or more master suites or is otherwise well-suited to a group of unrelated people living together. The owner or owners use the rental income to offset their mortgage costs while the (hopefully) appreciating property value serves as an investment.

Purchasing a duplex or quad-style multi-unit property also falls into this category. Becoming a landlord can make it easier to build your own micro-community where people live separately but together, all the while watching out for their neighbors. As an ambivert (someone who has both extrovert and introvert characteristics), this concept truly appeals to me. I love the idea of being able to close my door and retreat into my own space, knowing that I have neighbors just outside who are available for a chat, an impromptu meal or to keep an eye on things while I am gone.

New business models are also emerging. Home share businesses provide screening and matchmaking services that bring homeowners and renters together as housemates. Organizations such as HomeShare Vermont and Colorado startup Silvernest interview homeowners, look for compatible housemates, verify renter incomes, run background checks, provide lease agreements and offer support if problems develop. Homeowners usually pay a fee and then pocket the rental income, but different models are emerging as the concept gets refined. For-profit Silvernest markets itself as 'a long-term version of AirBNB coupled with Match.com for the AARP generation'. The company hopes to go national in 2018. Another Boulder startup, SeniorHomeshares.com, matches older homeowners who have more home than they need with potential housemates. House sharing appears to be a market with a lot of growth potential. Attention potential encore entrepreneurs: there is the core of a great business idea here!

If any of this sounds like something that you'd enjoy, the smart strategy is to try it on for size before you buy. Rent first, if possible, to get a real feel for your neighbors or housemates, the area, the weather, and whether there are opportunities for work and recreation that fit your needs. Make it a true test by making an effort to meet people and to fit into the community, so that you can be sure that your new home fits you.

I am about to launch on a similar adventure by moving into an active adult community for the first time. I did a lot of research on the types of people who are expected to buy in the specific community that I was considering to make sure that I wouldn't be too young or too solo (active adult communities traditionally attract a lot of couples). Neither appeared to be an issue. I wasn't searching for a free-standing home, but I do like the idea of having my own unattached four walls in the midst of a close-knit community. The floorplan and square footage was right, which is what mattered most, since I was ready to downsize even further than I already had. I had been thinking about moving to a more urban area, but also wanted to be close to the mountains and the hiking trails that I love. I already knew the area very well, since it is located less than a half hour from where I have lived for more than a decade and is close to some of my favorite hiking trails (though a further drive from shopping and services).

Despite all of my research, living in an active adult community will be an experiment and a learning experience for me. I am going in, eyes open, to try it on, see how it fits and get an insider's feel for what today's active adult community lifestyle is truly like. I suspect that it will fit pretty well by offering an ideal combination of privacy and social life, work and recreation (I work from a home office). I am planning to blog about the experience (www.activelyadult. com). Who knows? Active Solo Living may be the next book in the Solo series! Certainly my experience will be very useful to my future Entourage project. (Though I am hoping that another developer chooses to bring that concept to market long before I am ready to do so. I really just want to live there.)

Whatever we choose to call it – collaborative living, living in community, pocket neighborhoods, active adult or Entourage living – all of these housing styles are conducive to creating relationships and networks, reducing resource use and making it possible for solos and seniors (and those who are actively both) to thrive on their own. We really can achieve more, and enjoy life more, when we are surrounded by a sense of community that feels more intimate than a shared city or town, or even a neighborhood. Housing units are getting smaller and so are the informal communities that their owners are creating amongst themselves. It will be very exciting to see how housing develops in the coming years.

Community:

Create the Community You Crave

Independence and self-reliance are essential life skills for solos to develop. It is, however, equally important to build and maintain connections with other people – and not just as a strategy to avoid solitude or loneliness. All human beings need some sense of shared existence or network. Some need more than others, no doubt, but everyone needs human touchpoints. Abraham Maslow identified a sense of belonging as a fundamental need of all human beings – a building block that was as essential as food and water to survival.

Even the most introverted among us needs to have other people in our life. Even the most independent free-thinker needs to identify with some sort of group or tribe. It may seem like an oxymoron, but there is strength in numbers when it comes to living solo. We may enjoy living alone and spending time on our own, but no one wants to feel as if he or she is truly alone in the world. We need to know that help is available if we need it or want it. We like to know that someone will miss us if we fail to wake up, show up or come home on time (or ever). We crave connections, even if they are only with the clerk at the corner store or the neighbor who routinely walks by our front window. The interactions that we have with other humans are markers that add depth, pattern and rhythm to our lives. Sixteenth century poet John Donne wrote that 'no man is an island, entire of itself'. Similarly, no one person's life exists in a void or a vacuum.

We are all connected – and interconnected – in many different ways, whether we like it or not. What we truly crave, however, are emotional connections. Proximity alone is not enough.

When I talk about a sense of community, I am referring to meaningful connections that we share with other people, either through work or school, where we live or worship, or where we shop or choose to spend our time. Some will be familial or social or romantic relationships, others will be tenuous connections at best – yet they are connections just the same. Interactions with other humans are important. They provide us with information, social currency and opportunities to hone our communication skills. They keep us in touch with the world outside of our own four walls, prevent isolation and provide dimension to our day to day lives.

A strong social network also relieves stress, helps us recover from illness faster and can lead to a longer, happier life. People who have meaningful connections and relationships in their lives tend to also be more active and thus often healthier. An ongoing study by the Stanford Center on Longevity reported that, although feeling socially connected to others is critical to physical and mental health across age groups, traditional forms of social engagement are on the decline. According to a program summary: 'Younger and older Americans are not as likely to visit with neighbors or participate in community or religious organizations as their counterparts of 20 years ago'. Twenty percent of Americans also report that they do not have friends or family that they can rely on for help in an emergency. The most dramatic change was found among people in the 55 to 64-year-old age group who are 'engaging less with their communities, have fewer meaningful interactions with their spouses and weaker ties to family and friends'. Interaction and engagement are critical to creating a sense of community and support system.

Even the most casual social interaction can turn strangers into neighbors, neighbors into friends and friends into a potential support system. It is the opportunity for that interaction – and the willingness to act on it – which can seem difficult to find or embrace. Finding and making friends can be challenging for a variety of factors. Building a support system (typically only our closest friends are part of this system) can seem even more daunting. Think about the people who are currently in your life and what they mean to you, regardless of their role. It would probably be hard to imagine life without many of them, whether they are few or many (or perhaps sometimes too many). It's likely that you value each of these connections (assuming that they are positive) and if you don't, you are likely looking to replace them with relationships that are.

In her book *How We Live Now: Redefining Home and Family in the 21st Century*, social psychologist Bella DePaulo cites a *New York Times* story that outlined the conditions that help develop connections and close friendship: 'proximity, repeated and unplanned interactions, and a setting that encourages people to let their guard down and confide in each other'. This is exactly what I love about hiking in groups, which is my preferred 'connecting activity' of choice. You meet new people in a beautiful, stress-free natural setting and good things seem to happen naturally. When we are relaxed, we are approachable and when we are approachable, we are open to opportunity – and to sharing part of ourselves with someone else.

A group hike is an opportunity to get out into nature to enjoy the scenery, the fresh air, the challenge and the camaraderie. There is no agenda (other than finishing the hike) and conversations begin organically, based on 'Hi, how are you?', 'Where do you live?' or 'Have you hiked this trail before?' Hikers are good at casual conversation. They tend to be friendly and helpful and it can be surprisingly easy to find commonalities or shared interests that have nothing to do with hiking. It could be the setting (the great outdoors), the challenge (whether distance or elevation) or just the good feeling that comes from being part of a group, but conversations on the trail can often create a real connection. I have met a number of good friends this way and I love being part of the hiking community – not only in Arizona, but anywhere I go to hike. I have also made new friends while hiking in Colorado and France. It's not the place that really matters, it's the opportunity for a connection. As I get older, I find myself looking for more ways to proactively bring opportunities to meet new people with shared interests into my life. Moving into an active adult community is one of those strategies. I am actively 'tribe building' and I see living in an active adult community as a potentially powerful way to make a greater number of meaningful life connections.

There are a number of ways to create a shared sense of community. Many of them begin with shared interests, realities or connections. Housing is one very good way to do this and we have already looked at some of the options that can allow us to live 'alone but together', near other people, or physically together under the same roof with other people. A shared neighborhood or domicile creates a definitive connection that can evolve to become a closer relationship. This is a good thing when we get along with the people who live with or near us, and a not so good thing when we don't. New variations on 'living alone, together' seem to emerge every day, as people in search of community search for an option that works for them – often reshaping the way we live and the rules that we live by.

I recently bought a home in a brand-new active adult community that is located not too far from where I live now. The house is being built during the same period that I am writing this book. I had two concerns while I was deciding whether to buy into a resort-style community that, although not age restricted, will likely be mostly populated by people who are in the post-55 age bracket. The first was that I might be on the young side of the age group, which didn't bother me that much; the second that I might be a rare solo in a sea of married couples. I decided to take the plunge anyway, based on the research that I had been doing for this book (which told me that population trends were on my side regarding active retirement and solos), the percentage of single people that I was meeting in my hiking and other groups, and knowing that I would be able to make friends easily – solo or married – through the community's activity groups and classes. So far, my future neighbors whom I have met are in a similar age bracket to me (several are even younger) and are also solo, though many of them are fully retired (while I am still actively working). This tells me that, at the time that I move into my new home, I will have at least the beginnings of a posse who are in a similar stage of life as I am. I like knowing that the foundation for a new sense of community are taking shape at the same time that my new house is. It is a true example of 'building community' from the ground up.

Many people find a sense of community through their work. It's not unusual for workers to get emotional, social and intellectual rewards out of their jobs that go far beyond the paycheck and what it can buy, according to Chris Farrell, author of *Unretirement: How Baby Boomers Are Changing the Way We Think About Work, Community and the Good Life.* "The average Boomers' identity is wrapped up in work," writes Farrell. There's no doubt about that.

Often, so are their social and support networks. It's natural to forge connections with people with whom we spend a lot of time, often while working together toward shared goals. We learn things about them and they learn things about us, almost by osmosis. We belong to the work group and have an identity and role within it, even if we don't feel any other personal connection to its members, whether friendship or otherwise. People often have different sets of 'work friends' and 'personal friends' which help them maintain boundaries or pursue different interests. Whether you see work as a place to forge friendships or as an environment that is best left as strictly professional, it's likely that you derive a sense of belonging from going to work each day that satisfies more than your economic need to earn money to pay the bills.

This is one reason why many people may have a problem transitioning to retirement: they feel as if they are leaving their social network behind and, often, they are. It can be hard to maintain connections with work friends when you are no longer part of the day-to-day work environment and privy to the ever-changing rhythms of the workplace. Without shared connections, friendships can falter. Some retirees seek out part-time jobs for their social value as much as for the extra income. Working provides a reason to get up, get dressed and go out every day, as well as opportunities to interact with others and create new connections.

Shared activities are also a good basis for community. For me it has been hiking. I'm also planning to take up biking in the coming year. For you, it may be golf, or running or dancing or painting. When we join a community that is centered around an activity or an interest, or which provides an outlet for a passion that we want to develop, we surround ourselves with like-minded people who share that interest or passion. Both are the foundation for good connections. Activities (and activity groups) also provide us with opportunities to learn new skills and to add new interests to our lives. Hiking was never on my radar when I lived in Illinois (it's not very popular there) and I had lived in Arizona for nearly six years before I developed an interest in it. Then I discovered Meetup.

Meetup (www.meetup.com) is a great way to explore new interests and activities and meet people who share that interest wherever you may live or go. People join Meetup to meet other people who are actively looking to meet activity partners and friends. The explosion of Meetup groups across the United States (and globally) has made it easier to move to a new community, state or country knowing that you will always be able to find people who are interested in the same things that you are.

The internet in general has made the process of community building much easier, whether you are looking for new friends, a new love or just a Zumba class in a city that you are visiting. Social media sites and apps make it fast and easy to find activities, social groups and events as needed. Whenever someone complains about how social media mobile apps have created a world of people who are hunched over their phones or computers and living as introverts in online fantasy worlds, I start listing the ways in which I use those same sites and apps to find activities, classes and events that help me get out in the world and meet new people. Even better: I meet people whose paths might never have crossed with mine if it wasn't for an internet-based connection or social group. Technology has broadened my world in many positive ways.

Travel groups and clubs are another way to find and interact with people who share an interest in travel and who are also looking to explore the country or the world. I personally prefer to travel with someone or with a small group of people rather than by myself. I find that I am likely to be more adventurous, push my limits further, explore new places more fully and reach beyond my comfort zone when I have a partner in crime (or two) or the camaraderie (and support) of a small group of fellow travelers. On the other hand, I meet people all the time who swear by solo travel (traveling alone), say that they never feel lonely or threatened, and tell me that they meet interesting, friendly people everywhere they go. I have no doubt of this and I hope to one day put on my big girl pants and take a solo trip to see how that works for me. There is a large community of solo travelers out there, and I want to experience it for myself (and by myself) at some point.

Being part of an active community also helps you to keep moving and stay healthy by creating opportunities to stay (or get) active and involved. Call it competitiveness or peer pressure or whatever you like, I am more likely to push myself harder and further when hiking or otherwise working out in a group. Working out with other people (even total strangers) is also more fun because each workout, activity or session becomes a shared social event or experience. There's a connection – even if you never speak to another person in the room or on the hiking trail. The music, the exertion, the sweat and the experience are common denominators. Everyone feels as if they have been part of something – the same something, the same experience.

The obvious way to become part of an active community is to join a health club or participate in a community fitness program. A weekly class can be a far better way to make connections than at a gym or workout facility, where many people go to 'get away' from the real world while getting a workout (witnessed by the high number of ear buds and TV screens in most modern fitness centers). Meetup is also a good option, offering groups for just about any type of physical activity that you can think of (with regional variations). Finding a class or a group is often the easy part. Getting yourself to get dressed, get motivated and go for the first time can be (much) harder. What never fails to surprise me though is that, once I've taken that first step and actually shown up for a new activity or event, I always end up chatting with other participants and having a good time. If nothing else, a good fitness class or group will help you hone your social skills while getting a regular workout. It's a win-win, all the way around.

Volunteering and community involvement are both excellent ways to create a sense of community that also come with a real sense of satisfaction. When we help others, we help ourselves. When we lend our time, talents and expertise to a project or a cause or a need in our community, we link ourselves to that effort and its success. Recent retirees often plunge head first into community involvement as a way to recapture the sense of social involvement that they left behind with their job or career. Most non-profit organizations will tell you that adults in the 55 to 65 age group are their best targets for volunteers, donors and board members because they are high-energy, active individuals who have a lot of energy, experience and, often, resources of time and money to share.

Volunteering can also be good for your personal health. The Stanford Center on Longevity's Sitelines Project (launched with *TIME* magazine in 2016) is comparing Americans in six age groups with their counterparts from 15 to 20 years earlier. Among the initial findings is growing documentation that volunteering produces benefits to the physical and mental health of volunteers. According to a project report, more than 70 percent of people who volunteer prior to retirement continue to volunteer afterward – a percentage which is far higher than for those who had not volunteered while they were still working.

Getting involved in political campaigns is a good way to meet people with similar passion and perspective. So is volunteering for a non-profit which is working to address an issue that is important to you. There is no shortage of causes or campaigns that are perpetually looking for new volunteers or leaders. Becoming one of them can be the fastest way to meet potential new friends and add meetings, events or social activities to your calendar.

According to social psychologist and author Bella DePaulo, singles are much more likely to be active in their communities than married couples. "When people get married, they have less contact with their friends, their siblings and their neighborhood," she said in an interview with *The Christian Science Monitor*, adding that studies have shown that this is true even with people who are married but don't have any children. In a 2016 piece for *Nautilus*, DePaulo went on to write that singles are also more likely to 'host salons, take classes, go to rallies, organize unions, care for ageing friends and relatives, help raise kids and cultivate large, diverse social networks – often with more zeal and commitment than the married demographics they're displacing. Rather than tear us apart, the rising tide of solo dwellers is creating, sustaining and perhaps even strengthening, the ties that bind us.'

Sociologists Naomi Gerstel and Natalia Sarkisian also found that unmarried adults (solos) contribute far more to the community than society may give them credit for. Using published social survey and national data, they reported that never-married women are more politically active than their married counterparts and that, in general, solos are more engaged with their neighbors and have stronger networks of family and friends than married couples. In their book, *Nuclear Family Values, Extended Family Lives*, the duo argued that married people have become increasingly isolated because they perceive their relationship with their partner to be the only one that matters. This is only one reason why the social networks of unmarried respondents were found to be stronger than those of their married peers.

The bottom line? Creating a sense of community through volunteerism and service is likely to also be a good way to connect with other solos who are similarly altruistic and share your desire for a greater sense of connection and involvement.

There's no doubt that being part of a community provides benefits. The people in our networks are available to offer advice or support or to provide social interaction, get us out of the house and push us to try new things. We all want to know that we have someone we can call on in a crisis or a medical emergency, or when we need a ride, a helping hand or a shoulder to cry on. Solos can find it challenging to use outpatient services or obtain medical care at clinics which require a friend or family member to pick you up after the procedure. (Attention entrepreneurs: This is potentially a great opportunity to create a business around a clear and fast-growing market need.) Community can also be created among people who come together to help each other with the challenges of solo living. Think about the many ways that you can create community in your life. It's likely that you already know people who are looking for the same thing. Community is good for mind, body and spirt. It keeps us happy, engaged and active. Life as an active, healthy older solo is a very good thing. Ageing alone, without some sense of community in your life, is not.

Health:

Live Healthier, Not Just Longer

I am very much a quality versus quantity type of person, and especially when it comes to quality of life. I have no desire to live to a very old age unless I am also healthy and active. I realized this and became committed to better health for the first time when I turned 50. I have always been blessed with good health, despite some bad habits that stuck with me for most of my adult life. As I began to think about growing older – which is impossible to avoid on any milestone birthday – I realized that I needed to get healthy if I wanted to be healthy and stay healthy. I knew that staying healthy and active was the only way that I would be able to remain truly independent as I grew older – and when I say that, I am referring to physically and financially independent. I now know that the most important and valuable asset that I have is my health. Period. With it, I can accomplish anything. Without it, I could become reliant on others, the healthcare system or some other form of assistance. That is not the future that I want for myself (or for anyone) and I am doing everything that I can to actively avoid it.

Once I realized that I had to get healthy in order to stay healthy, I became proactive. I knew that I had to lay the groundwork for an active, healthy retirement long before my 70's or 80's rolled around. I had to get active, lose the weight, eat differently and learn how to stress less now – so I could be healthier and feel younger. I knew that it would be much harder to deal with or bounce back from a major illness than to get healthy and stay healthy.

My 93-year-old mother is a prime example. At the age of 84, she ended up in the hospital for nearly four months after a routine hospital procedure went wrong. Her esophagus was removed and she literally had to learn how to eat and swallow all over again. She went on to come home and make a full recovery and is still going strong today. She lives in a nice independent living facility, has friends, walks daily and still drives to the local community center. The surgeon and all of the hospital staff were amazed that a woman of her age could survive such an ordeal, much less make a full recovery, and they gave full credit to how healthy and strong she was going into the surgery.

Good inputs always create better outcomes. If you've ever had a knee or hip replacement, or really any major surgery, your doctor has probably told you to get yourself in the best shape possible *before* the surgery. The stronger you go in, the stronger you'll come out. The healthier you are, the healthier you are likely to stay. Now is the time to move your benchmark up, so that you age from a stronger base. Already retired? It is never too late to get started. Becoming healthy and active is something that only you can do for yourself. Do it now.

Solos have an advantage here. So much of becoming and staying healthy is related to what and how we eat. People who live alone are better able to control those choices, by what they buy and bring into their homes, and by what they choose to eat at each meal throughout the day. They can get up early to run, head out late to hike and leave workout equipment wherever they want to in their home. They can choose the activities and fitness plans that work best for them, without compromise. Solos are often also more active and social. Weekend plans often include group activities or classes, which can make it more fun to be active and to work out.

Of course, not all solos live alone and all married or coupled people aren't unhealthy eaters. If you are committed to being (or becoming) healthy, you will make it happen, and the best way to get that commitment can be to think about the future.

Higher levels of fitness in midlife have been linked to lower levels of dementia later in life, according to a 2013 study published in the *Annals of Internal Medicine*. Although a definitive link was not proven (healthy eating could also be a factor), it was generally concluded that physical fitness in middle age seems to be associated with a lower chance of developing dementia after age 65, providing yet another reason to become or stay physically fit in midlife.

Regular physical activity in midlife could also mean the difference between living independently (like my 93-year-old mother) or ending up in a care facility. If you are concerned about remaining independent as you age, now is the time to get focused on getting and staying fit and healthy. It really is all about the basics: Eat right, get exercise, sleep well, stay busy, and keep your mind engaged with people and projects. Retrain the way that you eat (I did). It's nowhere near as difficult as it sounds. We've all heard or read this same advice throughout our lives, but it doesn't really begin to hit home for most of us until we start to see the first signs of ageing. Or have a friend or associate who gets sick or dies too early. Or watch our parents or siblings begin to fail. Suddenly all of those 'get fit' articles get real.

One of the real game-changers for me was watching the PBS documentary 'In Defense of Food', which was based on the book of the same name by author and self-proclaimed food activist Michael Pollan. Pollan's simple, common-sense mantra – Eat Food, Not Too Much, Mostly Plants – made a lot of sense to me. I had worked to eliminate a lot of things out of my cabinets, my fridge and my life since turning 50, and learned to crave (yes, crave) salads and other good-for-you foods. (It is surprising how you really can retrain your cravings and taste buds.) I now eat differently than I did even five years ago, and it's reflected in my energy levels, my skin quality and my weight. I now weigh less than I did in my 40's and I am, without question, in better overall shape than I have ever been in my adult life. My new knowledge has been literally life-changing. Learn more about Pollan at www.michaelpollan.com.

Another game-changer: Making exercise and movement part of my life and more than a daily routine. I bought my first FitBit two years ago. It is the Zip model, which clips into my pocket and which I wear all day, every day. It's not the most accurate fitness tracker on the market, but it is the least obtrusive (versus bracelet models). This model counts your steps (and miles) and then uploads them to a program which keeps track of how far I have walked or hiked every day, week, month and year. There are a wide variety of fitness trackers, whether wearable or phone app, on the market that do the same thing (and much more). It is surprising how quickly a fitness tracker becomes part of your life, prompting you to walk and move more, whether you are competing against yourself or in challenges with friends. I am always bummed when I am halfway through my morning walk or hike and realize that I left my FitBit at home. I also find myself parking further away from a destination or taking stairs more often, to get more steps in. For less than $50, it was a great investment in my health and wellbeing.

I am also here to tell you that all of those articles on eating right and exercising well are true. That's what really works, as boring (or disappointing) as it may sound. Since I eliminated certain foods from my life (soda, most dairy, processed foods), starting eating healthier (more fruits and vegetables, better protein and healthier fats), learned how to identify when I was eating out of boredom and not hunger (too often), and learned portion control (this actually proved to be the biggest factor), I began to lose weight without dieting. I changed the way that I shop, eat and think about food and that – along with hiking, walking and minimal other exercise – changed the shape of my body. If someone had told me that these changes would have produced the results that they have this easily (and it hasn't felt hard at all), I would have laughed at them (and did). I never believed any of that 'eat less and exercise more' stuff, but you know what? It's true, and it's not hard. My new reality (better diet, more movement and exercise) is going to help me stay active and healthy for many years to come – and hopefully for the rest of my life.

I know that my new lifestyle would be much harder to maintain if I was living with someone who had different eating or food shopping habits. I'm no saint. If something is in the house, I will be tempted by it and will probably eat it. Living alone does make all of this easier (you can't eat what you didn't buy, and what you didn't buy isn't in the house), which is another benefit of being (or at least living) solo: control over your living environment. There are certain things (cookies, chips, etc.) that I just don't bring home from the grocery store. Having like-minded roommates or partners could probably also work, if they were similarly motivated to eat healthy. The best roommates, life partners or love interests are almost always going to be people who share our views on health, food and fitness.

Housemates or roommates may become a necessary reality for many people as they get older. Physical issues will develop as our bodies age. We may find it harder to get around or to reach up for things. It can be harder to navigate shopping (carrying), driving (eyesight) and staying fit (the exercises of our youth may be too hard on older knees or backs). Even those of us who have lived on our own for a while, have become good at it and want to continue living that way will likely have to make adjustments as time goes by, regardless of how healthy we may be. There is an entire industry based around 'ageing in place' and helping people stay in their current homes or living arrangements as long as possible, whether through home improvements, in-home assisted medical and non-medical services, or other services for hire that can help take care of driving, shopping and companionship needs on demand.

Health is the part of ageing that scares many of us the most. My two greatest fears are 1) outliving my money or my ability to earn more money; and 2) losing my health and my mobility, and becoming dependent on other people or institutions for care. Actually, I am more worried about the second than the first. As long as my health holds out, I should always be able to find a way to earn some income. I know that. I also know that living solo requires a lot of energy. That energy tends to diminish as we get older. The idea of living with others in some sort of shared housing arrangement becomes more appealing to me with each year – not just for its social aspects, but also for the peace of mind that would come from knowing that others would be nearby to help in the event of a medical emergency or illness.

Insurance can also help in those situations. The cost of healthcare, let along long-term care, has blown through the roof and very few people have the resources to be able to pay for a major medical event or a long-term stay in an assisted living or rehab facility. Yes, they offer insurance for this. No, I don't know enough about it to write about it. There are plenty of experts who can explain the pros and cons of long-term care and/or disability insurance. Ditto on Medicare, which has become increasingly complicated. Medicare does not cover all of your healthcare costs. There will also be deductibles, co-payments, premiums and co-insurance to pay, depending on the plan and the circumstances. Extra coverage may be needed. I know that by 60, I need to become conversant in all of the options and programs so that I can make an informed choice when it is time. Learn how Medicare works and how it can work for you. Ditto on Social Security.

Consider it part of your changing life to know everything there is to know about programs that are designed to assist you as you get older. Then also make sure that you have a living will and that any other healthcare directives for care or support, or powers of attorney are up to date and in place. True independence comes from knowing that your healthcare needs will be taken care of and respected, even (especially) as your health fades. These are important matters for anyone to tend to – solo or otherwise. Never assume that the people who are close to you know your wishes, or will be willing to honor them when the time comes.

Lifestyle:

Are You Ready for Retirement?

The greatest challenge of retirement may come from rebalancing the way that you use and value your time. What used to be a carefully orchestrated schedule of work, chores, social life and other responsibilities can quickly become a blank canvass of open days, lots of possibilities, and time, lots of time.

Many retirees underestimate the amount of time that they will have available once they stop working. Most of us will have roughly 16 waking hours each day to fill in some way. You can accomplish a lot in 16 hours, no doubt, but it can also seem like a lifetime if no meaningful activity is part of your day. Structure and purpose give us a reason to get up in the morning, whether we are going to work or headed to the beach.

Most of us realize that we have to think strategically about how we are going to first save, and then pay for, retirement. But do we think enough about how we are going to spend our time? Some people enter retirement with a full-blown plan. Others are determined to let each day shape itself. Still others find empty days to be even more stressful than going to work. The thought of a '30-year vacation' may sound good as we look toward the future, but retirement rarely works out that way. Too much free time can cause dissatisfaction or even depression in formerly busy people.

It appears that individuals who continue working past 65 tend to be happier, whether they do so by choice or need. A Brookings Institute analysis of Gallup World Poll data for 2010 – 2013 revealed a 'happiness premium' among older workers who were working full time or voluntarily employed in part-time work. Late-life workers (e.g. people working past the traditional retirement age of 65) were typically happier and more satisfied with their health than their fully retired counterparts. Stimulation and satisfaction were two of the benefits that were cited. Purpose was another.

The transition from working to retirement is not an easy one. "Few people realize how much of their identity is wrapped up in what they do for a living and how difficult it can be to wake up one day and not follow the routine that's become habit over the past 30-plus years," according to financial planner Mike Branham. "It takes time to adjust."

Retirement represents a change in status, schedule and, often, also friendships, economics and health. It's a time when we start thinking about how fast time goes by, where we're headed, what we'd still like to achieve or do, and how we want to spend our remaining time. It's a time when many people make a commitment to live with more purpose.

Living in community is all about seeking and creating meaningful connections with other people. Living in retirement usually becomes focused on living with purpose. We all want to have a sense of purpose in our lives. Purpose provides the motivation, and the excitement, that keeps us moving forward toward our goals, whatever they may be. Social connections are an essential element to enjoying retirement. The people who are part of our life help provide a sense of community and a sense of purpose. Making an effort to meet new people and make new friends will fulfill both needs, while also helping to fill an empty calendar.

Most Americans spend much of their careers waiting for retirement, but is retirement always 'better'? A 2011 poll of 1,254 people over the age of 50 conducted by NPR, the Robert Wood Johnson Foundation and the Harvard School of Public Health found that 44 percent of retirees considered their overall quality of life to be about the same as when they were still working full time. Only 29 percent of respondents reported that leaving the workforce had made their life 'better'.

How can that be? Are Americans spending most of their lives working toward a retirement fantasy that doesn't exist? No, but there are a number of common misconceptions that many people hold about retirement. According to the study, 55 percent of the respondents expected retirement to be less stressful than work, but only 39 percent reported that they actually had less stress in their post-retirement lives. This could be due to false expectations about health or finances, according to Gillian SteelFisher, an assistant director with the Harvard Opinion Research Program. "Almost a quarter (24 percent) said that they faced more stress in retirement," she noted. Thirty-five percent said that their stress levels remained the same.

Travel is a common retirement goal, but 34 percent of retirees said that they travel less than they did in the past and 35 percent spend as much time on vacations as they did while they were working. Many people (68 percent) expect to have more time for sports, hobbies and volunteering in retirement, but 43 percent reported having about the same amount of time available, or even less (20 percent). This can include making time for exercise. More time means more time available for the gym or the hiking trail, right? Not always. A third of retirees said that they get less exercise than when they got up and went to work every day. Just over 40 percent said that they racked up about the same amount of exercise in an average day.

Health can be the wild card. Most older workers (69 percent) expect to maintain their current level of health, at least in the first half of their retirement, according to the Harvard School of Public Health. That can be a slippery slope, as we all know. Only 43 percent of retirees reported that their health was as good as it was five years earlier. Let's face it. Many of us can probably say the same thing. That's why I am a firm believer in being as active as possible, and in taking as many active vacations as I can manage now, while my health (and my knees) are still strong. I am not going to wait for 'retirement' or some future day when there is no guarantee that my health will be as good as it is today.

The biggest challenge for many retirees comes in trying to maintain their current standard of living post-career. People are surprisingly, and sometimes unrealistically, optimistic about how easy it will be to afford paying for a lifestyle that will not only be similar to what they enjoy today, but which is also likely to include more activities, travel, eating out and other expenses – with increasing healthcare costs being one of the highest. Many people may choose to spend the first years of retirement traveling but, as the years pass, travel spending often decreases as healthcare and family-related costs go up.

"People are not looking forward enough in terms of the health issues they will face and the actual financial income they are really going to have," explained Robert Blendon, a professor of health policy and political analysis at the Harvard School of Public Health. "Healthcare expenses are a major problem." One in five survey respondents (20 percent) said that they were having trouble paying for healthcare. The biggest key to a happy retirement may be good health. Without it, money becomes an even greater issue.

Being solo can be a plus in retirement. Married couples face the biggest adjustments to retirement. One in three couples can't agree on the lifestyle they want to lead. How to save for retirement, and then how to spend once retired can also cause conflict and require a lot of compromise. Solos have to work harder to save for retirement, but they also have the benefit of knowing that they are working toward their vision of what retirement should be, not a collage or compromise. According to the Census Bureau, women, on the average, live six years longer than men and 60 percent of women over the age of 65 are single, widowed or divorced. Married women who make compromises or lifestyle-altering decisions with their spouses in the early years of retirement often have to live with those choices later, as solos. This is another reason why it is important to plan for a solo future, no matter how happily coupled you may currently be. One of you is going to end up on his/her own eventually.

Rebalancing How You Live

Retirement should be about moving forward and embracing new possibilities and opportunities – and not about leaving something behind. Think of retirement as rebalancing, reinventing or re-imagining, rather than retiring, and it is far more likely to be a positive experience.

If age alone is no longer the benchmark, and 65 is just another number, then how do you know when you're ready for retirement? Set finances aside for the moment and think about what will be left in your life once you take work out of the equation. How will you view your identity? Do you already have hobbies or volunteer activities that you are actively involved in? How often do you get together with friends? Do you have friends who are not just 'work friends'? Do you exercise? Is it often enough? Do you travel? Do you want to get started? Do you have someone to travel with if you don't want to travel alone? Do you have goals or dreams that have nothing to do with earning a paycheck, or that you have been putting off until there was 'more time' to realize them? There are a lot of unknowns and a lot of uncertainty that comes with any major life change and retirement is a very big life change. Are you ready for a radical shift in your daily life?

Many people aren't and it's becoming more common for older workers to approach retirement in stages, by gradually reducing their hours, or by switching from full-time work to a part-time job. Not everyone wants to stop working completely. Many just want to work differently. Surveys by the American Association of Retired Persons (AARP) have shown that more than 70 percent of older workers want to continue working in some way. Respondents placed a high value on meaningful work that will keep them engaged, allow them to 'reinvent themselves' and show the world (and themselves) that they haven't 'given up on life'. An impressive 86 percent reported that they believe that staying in the workforce will keep them healthy and active.

"Many times, work is what you do and not so much who you are," wrote Osher Lifelong Learning Institute executive director Catherine Frank in a *Kiplinger* article on ageing. "Retirement is an opportunity to create a life that reflects more closely with who you are."

The key is to identify a mix of activities that provide meaning and integrate them into your life. This could include income-producing or volunteer work, classes, activities, community service and more time for friends and family.

And of course, there's 'those questions' that each of us is supposed to ask ourselves periodically to ensure that we are making the most of our limited time on earth: If money wasn't an issue, how would you live? If your doctor told you that you have just five years to live, would you change your life and how would you do it? If your doctor told you that you have six months to live, how would you spend them? Questions like these are meant to help us focus on what is most important to us (though you could argue that the limited timeframe skews the answers). In any event, it's good to know what your answers might be so that you don't have to start from scratch following some bad news from your doctor. Hopefully, that will never be the case, but your efforts could give your life new energy.

The answers that we get from thinking about 'worst case scenarios' are helpful in making sure that we are living life with 'purpose', and that we aren't putting off our goals or desires until some future date, when we will either be retired, or wealthy, or (hopefully) both. Time passes faster as we get older, and we begin to realize how finite it is. The best time to realize our goals and get out there to do the things that we want to do is while we are healthy, happy and mobile. We will enjoy everything more, and our bucket lists will be shorter should bad news befall us at some point in the future. Whenever we postpone something, we risk seeing it never experienced, realized or achieved. Or as Pablo Picasso wrote: 'Only put off until tomorrow what you are willing to die having left undone.' I have this framed and hanging on the wall in my office.

When we move toward retirement, our focus begins to shift from what we are to who we want to be and what we want our life to be like, beyond work. Successfully making this shift means creating a life portfolio or menu which potentially incorporates a balance of work, learning, recreation, travel, volunteer or other altruistic efforts, family, friends and personal fulfillment. Visualize your life portfolio as a pie chart that allocates time and attention to the pursuits that you value most, based on their priority. The exercise alone will force you to think about what is important to you.

What does your 'ideal retirement' look like? What types of activities will it include and in what ratios? Think about it, write it down and refine it. Draw a chart. Create a visual. This is your opportunity to begin creating a vision and a plan for how you want to spend the rest of your time on earth, whether you choose to measure it in years or decades. Think about the balance that you want to create between work, play, community, family and other interests. This is about rebalancing and reimagining, not retirement. This is not about the end of a chapter. It is about envisioning a new beginning: the time when you focus on quality of living, and not just quantity or accumulation.

In his book, *Flourish*, author Martin E. P. Seligman wrote 'Wellbeing is a combination of connection, engagement and purpose, and meaning.' Having a sense of purpose adds direction and meaning.

It also can add years to your life, according to a 2014 study published in *Psychological Sciences*. Researchers from Carleton University in Ottawa, Ontario and the University of Rochester in New York traced the physical and mental health of more than 7,000 American adults ages 20 to 75 for 14 years. They found that those who felt that they had a purpose or direction in life outlived those who did not.

Think about what your ideal retirement looks like and consider the practical requirements of your vision. What will it take to achieve your goals and to live the way that you would like to live? This is how you create a plan to make it happen, one step at a time.

I wrote about visualizing goals and getting them on paper in my first book, *Be the Bulb!* (2009, Herlife Publishing). What works for me may also work for you. Committing pen to paper (or fingers to keyboard) is essential. Writing down goals makes them concrete and real and creates a stronger level of commitment. Using images can also be very powerful. I am the proud owner of a full set of Sharpies and an oversized artist's drawing pad, tools that I use to draw charts and colorful lists that help me think through and define my goals for all parts of my life. Different colors also make it easier to create emphasis, and to see how different elements overlap or relate to each other. Color really does bring concepts to life.

Create a pie chart image of what retirement or a 'life portfolio' looks like to you. Start by making a list of the things that are most important for you to have in your life. Include your personal and professional development goals (yes, you may still have them), as well as any entrepreneurial business goals. Sample categories could include: personal, professional, financial, physical and spiritual needs and goals. The importance of the items in each list will give you a feel for their proportions in your pie chart.

Play with the proportions of the elements until it feels right to you. Keep it handy and in a location where you can see it and refer to it whenever you feel like you are moving sideways instead of forward, or are stuck in one spot. The chart will remind you of what you are working toward and what your priorities are.

Goals get you to success. They point you in the right direction and provide you with mile markers to help you gauge your progress. Break larger goals into smaller steps to make them more easily attainable. Napoleon Hill said it best: 'A goal is a dream with a deadline.' Attach a timeline to the realization of your goals to keep you moving forward. We build momentum when our goal is in sight, or feels as if it is within reach.

You are planning a lifestyle. Goals are guidelines, but should remain flexible. Life changes, often, and the key to keeping stress at bay is to be flexible and roll with the changes. Retirement is a journey, not a destination. It should also always be a work in progress. Be sure to take time to stop and think about whether what you are doing is going to get you to where you want to go. If not, adjust. Retirement, more than any other time in our lives, is when we are most able to go with the flow and adapt.

Ross Levin, a certified financial planner in Edina, MN sees retirement as a '50-50 lifestyle that is fueled by passion'. "When your interests align with your work, there is nothing from which to retire," he wrote. Once we do retire, it can be easy to justify taking a lower-paying part-time job that fulfills a passion or lifelong dream. Think of it this way, wrote Levin: "You could earn $10,000 a year in your fulfilling work on a ski slope or in a national park or down in the Florida Keys. That's the equivalent of having $250,000 in investment assets, assuming the 4 percent withdrawal rule" (which is considered a basic guideline for taking money out of your retirement savings). A part-time job that appears to provide a low income can actually have a lot of value, both personally and financially. You might scoff at working far below your former salary, but earning a $20,000 annual income from a job which allows you to do something that you are passionate about is the equivalent of having $500,000 in assets (plus or minus the tax liabilities). That's something to think about.

This was a real eye opener for me. The value of work, and money, changes significantly in retirement, if only by what it can represent and provide (satisfaction as well as income). If nothing else gives you hope about your future financial security, this should. If you choose to continue working, look for an opportunity that will allow you to pursue a passion, realize a life goal, learn a new skill, expand your social network, or get out and give back to the community. It really is like having money in the bank.

Dare to Enjoy Being Solo

The greatest concern that some people may have is whether they, as solos, will be capable of facing retirement on their own (aka 'alone'). They may be worried about being bored, lonely or lacking an adequate support system should health or money issues raise their ugly heads.

If you've gotten this far, you know that there are many ways to create a sense of community and the support system that often comes with that. You've also learned that being solo has very little to do with being 'alone' and that it is certainly no guarantee of loneliness. Life is what we make of it, whether we are solo or partnered, male or female, parents or childless. It is all about perspective. Dare to be solo and strong. Give yourself permission to embrace a solo retirement and the many opportunities that it can offer. Make this time in your life all about you. You've earned it.

There is no reason to be or feel isolated in this day and age, when both high-tech and low-tech opportunities to connect with people exist all around us. When the walls start closing in (and they may, from time to time), take action to meet new people and add more social interaction into your life. Take an exercise or a Zumba class. Join a gym or a hiking group. Volunteer for a cause or a campaign. Check out continuing education classes at your local community college, either to take or to teach. Example: The Bernard Osher Foundation supports a national lifelong learning network for older adults (50 and up) which includes Learning Institutes on 119 campuses across the U.S. Its National Resource Center is headquartered at Northwestern University (my alma mater). You can learn about current programs, including scholarship and fellowship opportunities, at www.osherfoundation.org.

Maybe you have recently found yourself Suddenly Solo for the first time. This is a good opportunity for you to learn how to acquire some of the solo survival skills that I listed on page 30. Tackle them one step at a time. Each will be empowering. Going out on your own can be a big step for a lot of people. I still don't like to go out to dinner or events by myself and I have been living solo for more than a dozen years. Each time I do venture out solo, however, it gets easier and definitely more fun.

Solo travel may also seem daunting at first, but it is one of the fastest growing trends in the tourism industry. Nearly 25 percent of people traveled alone on most of their overseas leisure vacation, up from 15 percent in 2013, according to the *2015 Visa Global Travel Intentions Study.* The study included travelers from 25 countries. Solo travel is even more popular among first-time travelers, with 37 percent of first-timers heading out on their own (up from 16 percent in 2013).

Adventure travel company G Adventures reports that about 11 percent of its travelers go solo, which is an increase of 134 percent over 2008. The age of their average solo customer is 54 and rising. Americans and British travelers are the most likely to venture out solo. Apparently, they're more adventurous.

Here's the most interesting part: solo travel isn't just for solos. Today's solo traveler is as likely, if not more so, to be married or in a committed relationship. It is not uncommon for a couple to include a traveler and a homebody, or to have one partner who has more flexibility to plan a getaway than the other. According to AARP, 53 percent of American solo travelers who are 45 or older are married and 39 percent are single or divorced. That makes solo travel a great way to meet many different types of people.

These trends are also helping to slowly eliminate the dreaded 'single supplement' that solo travelers have been forced to pay for many years. Some fees are being lowered or dropped completely and more packages are being marketed to people who want to travel solo. Cruise companies, long notorious for up-charging singles every step of the way, are adding more cabins that are smaller and dedicated to solo travelers, thus doing away with single surcharges that often added 10 to 100 percent more to the standard cabin rate.

Traveling as a solo in a small group of unrelated solo travelers is also a growing niche. For the record, these are groups of solo travelers who prefer to travel with other solos (rather than alone). They are typically looking for company, not a partner or a hookup. There is a real business opportunity for companies to better serve this market. I know because I am the target market. As I like to say, I have friends who have money and no time, and friends who have time and no money. The result is that it can be pretty tough to come up with a travel partner when I have an urge to hit the road or the airport. I personally prefer to travel with friends or in small groups of other travelers, even if I don't know anyone in the group. Finding companies that put groups of like-minded travelers together has been difficult at best. There are more choices in the adventure sector, where companies like Backroads, Overseas Adventure Travel (OAT) and National Geographic Travel offers 'solo traveler' versions of their most popular trips. At OAT, 80 percent of their solo travelers are women. The company was also a leader in eliminating single supplements and does not charge solo travelers a premium on any of its trips.

Embracing your solo-ness (whether at home or on the road) has nothing to do with being alone. There are plenty of ways to find the like-minded people or partners whom you may want in your life. We've already talked about online activity sites like Meetup.com, where you can join an existing group or choose to start your own on a topic or activity that you are truly passionate about. The cost to start and host a new Meetup group is right around $100 a year and, as the administrator or organizer, you will get to 'meet' and interact with everyone who chooses to join your group. It's also smart to find co-organizers early on, to help plan events and manage the workload. If you have an interest in a certain activity or topic, the chances are pretty good that others do too. It has never been easier to find them at home or afar using easy online tools.

See your solo-ness as the opportunity that it is and embrace it. Ignore any naysayers or people who may encourage you to 'couple up' if you have no interest in doing so. We live in a couple-driven society and there are bound to be people who will wonder why you're single, or try to 'fix you up' so that you 'won't be alone'. Don't feel defensive or pressured to do anything that you don't want to do. You are part of a rising demographic. Nearly half of all American adults are single. Once you've been on your own for a while, you'll appreciate why it's the fast-growing demographic in the country. Being solo brings a lot of freedom with it.

Focus on friendship. Being solo makes it easier to find more time to do things, and to do them on your terms. Get out and meet new activity partners, create meaningful new friendships or spend more time with your existing circle. Your time is yours to schedule.

Enjoy your freedom and indulge your passions. Try something that you have always wanted to do. Travel wherever you want. Live in a tiny house. Take up late-night baking or writing. Obsess over a garden. Get outdoors and explore on your own. In other words, do whatever you want to when you want to do it. If you're like me, you never really had this freedom while you were busy working, taking care of a household or a business, and/or involved in relationships that included spouses, significant others or children. This is your time. Being self-centered is good, not selfish. It means that you are focused on your needs and what is good for you. Never apologize for taking care of your needs, potentially for the very first time.

Celebrate that there is no longer any need to compromise. Being in a relationship usually requires discussion and often compromise on even minor decisions. Often, we don't realize how much we were giving up until we are solo and living on our own. Live the way you want to, and on a schedule that works for you. Buy and cook the types of foods you want to eat. Watch the shows and movies that you enjoy. Know that when you put something away (or leave it out), it will stay there until you do something with it again. Relationships can add many good things to our lives but they also add stress, compromise, rigidity and, let's face it, more than a little predictability. Spontaneity can be pretty tough to pull off. Solos only have just one schedule to consult: their own. That provides flexibility, which makes it possible to explore new opportunities and be spontaneous. Leverage both to discover and create a lifestyle that you really enjoy.

Solo by Chance: Looking for Love

After three marriages and a number of interesting but ill-fated relationships, I have (finally) fully embraced being solo. Oh, don't get me wrong. I love being in a satisfying relationship as much as the next person and I am always open to the possibility of meeting someone who has similar energy, passion and a complementary perspective on love, work and life, but I don't see myself getting married again or even living with anyone whom I am romantically and sexually involved. It took much of my adult life to realize it, but I now know that I really am at my happiest, my most creative and my most productive when I am not married or cohabitating with someone. I love having my own personal space to live, work, write, relax and entertain in. I love being able to welcome friends into a comfortable, inviting environment that is truly a reflection of me. I cherish the time that I spend alone and rarely, if ever, feel lonely. I am very much an ambivert: a person who has introverted tendencies and is (very) comfortable by herself, but who also does very well in social settings and with other people. Living alone allows me to embrace either side of my personality as I please and as the mood strikes me, with no compromise needed. I can retreat into the comfort of my home, or go out into the world headfirst and be a social butterfly. Either one is just a different version of me.

Let's face it though, not everyone who is solo wants to remain solo. There is a multi-billion-dollar industry dedicated to bringing single people together to date and potentially mate. One of the fastest segments of this industry is the over-50 age group. As we

115

get older, the thought of ageing alone – or worse yet, dying alone – starts to move front and center in our consciousness, making many people uncomfortable with their solo status. Often the search for love is really just a search for companionship. Some people are simply not comfortable with being on their own or with living alone. Many people worry about getting sick and having to deal with it on their own (and even though there are many other ways to find support).

Still others see marriage as a strategy: to gain financial security, domestic services or a potential caregiver in the years ahead (the 'nurse with a purse' strategy employed by some older men). Study after study has shown that older widowers tend to remarry faster than widows in their age group. In his book, *Going Solo*, Eric Klinenberg points out that only two percent of widows and 20 percent of widowers over 65 remarry. Older women who have friends and active social lives are the least likely to remarry: only one in six are interested in potentially pairing up again, according to Rutgers University sociologist Deborah Carr.

Men, faced with the prospect of caring for themselves and their homes, often after decades of blissful ignorance regarding most domestic chores, see remarriage as a way to assure their continued well-being. Both men and women, accustomed to waking up and spending most of their lives with their former spouse, may find the prospect of living alone daunting – even if their marriages had been unhappy or mostly silent – and they race to replace their former mate with another warm body. For many of these people, being alone seems worse than being (and living) with bad company. Traditionally, it works the other way around (it is definitely better to be alone than in bad company).

Some women (and yes, it's more often women) see marriage as a financial strategy – a guarantee that they won't end up penniless or on the streets (the dreaded bag lady syndrome). They hope to find a mate who will provide for them and their needs, either fully or in part, so that they don't have to worry about retirement, running out of money or returning to work. There's a big flaw in that plan. Marriage is no guarantee of financial security, happiness or companionship. Divorce is far too easy and 'grey divorce' has been on the rise for decades. Getting remarried too quickly can also put what assets you do have at risk if things don't work out. A pre-nuptial agreement should be standard operating procedure for anyone who is considering getting married again – whether for the first time, the second or the sixth. Think very carefully before co-mingling your assets with anyone. Your financial future is at stake.

And does getting re-married really make sense in the first place? You do not have to be married to be committed to someone or to live with someone. You do not have to be with someone to be happy and secure. You do not have to with anyone to be comfortable with your own company. This is what giving yourself permission to be solo is all about: Be comfortable with yourself and be able to provide for yourself so that any decisions that you make (whether romantic, financial or otherwise) will be made from a position of *strength* and *not need*. If you get nothing else from this book, please take that message to heart. There is strength in being solo: financial strength, personal strength and physical strength. Embrace that, don't run from it. Take responsibility for your own well-being, financial security, happiness and health. That is the only real way to create security in your life.

There is no denying that marriage does offer some benefits – more than 1,000 Federal tax benefits, according to social psychologist Bella DePaulo, who wrote in her 2006 book *Singled Out* that when a single person and a married couple filing jointly report the same taxable income, there is never a marriage penalty. It is single people who always pay more. Single people also subsidize married people in many other ways, reported DePaulo, citing discounts for couples on auto insurance, club memberships and travel packages that leave singles paying full price. Married couples also tend to earn significant discounts on health insurance.

Marriage offers definite financial and legal benefits. Married couples filing jointly enjoy higher income tax exemptions and can write off more charitable deductions. A lower-earning spouse can bring down the tax rates for both partners, so that the higher-earning spouse pays less than he or she would have if solo. Marriage also allows a non-working spouse to open an IRA and save for 'retirement', even while not working. The IRA of a deceased spouse can be rolled over to the surviving spouse tax-free. There are also opportunities for tax-free gift giving and estate planning. The list goes on and on.

Spouses also have access to each other's Social Security benefits and health insurance benefits. They have the right to enter a hospital room or make decisions about healthcare and end of life matters for their spouse – rights that domestic partners or even life-long friends do not have. They can inherit tax-free and without question in most states, often even when no will exists. A solo person may work a lifetime and then die, leaving his or her Social Security benefits unused and thrown back into the general fund. Only spouses can step in to collect death or other remaining benefits.

You might think that this 'marriage bonus' would lead some people to get married just for the tax deductions, or to ensure that their partner (or someone close to them) has the legal authority to carry out their healthcare or end of life wishes without question. There could be some merit to 'unromantic marriage' as a financial and legal strategy, which was far more common than marrying for love until the twentieth century rolled around. In her latest book, *How We Live Now*, DePaulo identified a rising trend in couples who are LAT (living apart together) – some married, others solo but committed. Many of us know married couples who make long distance or bi-coastal relationships and living arrangements work. For some of these people, marriage may be a strategy as much as a sign of commitment. Time will tell how the trend develops. It is likely to continue to grow, just as non-traditional households, living arrangements and personal relationships are continuing to diversify and grow.

Sexual need and desire have always brought potential partners together. Age does little to put out that fire, especially in the age of Viagra, Cialis and hormone therapies for both men and women. You don't have to be married, partnered or in a committed relationship to realize the benefits of a satisfying sex life. Just keep in mind that, although birth control may no longer be an issue, practicing safe sex to avoid STDs and other sexually-transmitted diseases is more important than ever. Being active means also being proactive to stay healthy. It is also a responsibility that you have to every partner.

There is a very impressive list of benefits that regular orgasm offers to men and women beyond sexual release and enjoyment. Regular orgasm boosts mood, by releasing feel-good chemicals like endorphins, dopamine and serotonin. Regular release also relieves anxiety, reduces stress, enhances creativity and improves work performance. Scientific studies have documented the physical benefits of regular orgasm, which include a boosted immune system, higher levels of immunoglobulin A, or IgA, an antibody that fends off infection, improved digestion and blood flow, lowered blood pressure, a lower risk of heart disease and lowered mortality rates. Really.

Solo sex can also help you sleep better, get fit, detox your body and practice natural pain relief. Your appearance will also benefit from shinier hair, glowing skin and a reduced appetite. Sound too good to be true? It's not. The research on the benefits of regular masturbation and orgasm is voluminous and growing. (How do I know? Because the many health and ageing benefits of solo sexuality are potentially the topic of my next book!)

The news gets even better as we get older. Orgasms improve with age. According to the LELO Global Sex Survey, the older women get, the more satisfaction they report, with more than 75 percent of those over 60 claiming that their sexual satisfaction is higher than ever before. The American Journal of Medicine also found that sexual satisfaction in women increases with age. Orgasm can also ease menopause and its symptoms, and reduce incontinence. It also promotes healthy estrogen levels that can help protect against osteoporosis and heart disease. In men, regular orgasm can reduce the risk of prostate cancer and rare, but still deadly, breast cancer.

You do not have to be in a relationship or have a partner to realize the many benefits of regular orgasm. Solo sexuality (masturbation) provides sexual pleasure for people who do not have partners or who have chosen to abstain from sexual activities with another person for health or emotional reasons. Contrary to the out of date myths and warnings, masturbation is healthy, normal and very good for you. It's a practical way to be very proactive about your health and appearance at any age.

Although it's clear that it doesn't take two to be happy, financially fit or even sexually satisfied, there's no question that there are some solos who just don't want to go it alone, whether they are Suddenly Solo, never coupled or still actively in search of 'the one'. There are plenty of options for people who are single but unwilling to embrace a 'party of one' philosophy to find the people and partners they want in their lives. It has never been easier to go 'looking for love', or to find love and belonging in new and non-traditional ways. Definitions of partnership, family, friendship and even marriage have changed and continue to evolve. It is often as we get older, and after a lifetime of experience, that we become far more open to redefining the types of relationships that we will consider.

Planning Ahead:

Who Will Be There for Me?

One of the things that I've learned through the process of writing this book is that solo comes in a lot of different variations. Much like blended families, modern living arrangements and multi-generational workplaces, one size does not fit all, or describe all, any longer (as if it ever did.) Solos may not be married or in a committed relationship, but many if not most of them have families, friends or co-workers who are part of their lives and who care about their wellbeing. Ditto for childless solos, who – despite silly stereotypes – are not doomed to die alone in their rooms without anyone to notice that they're gone.

Let's face it though. If you live alone and are childless, or have grown children or other family who live far away or are out of touch, you have likely thought about what will happen when you die – especially if you die while home alone. Who will notice that you are missing? Who will find you? Who will take care of the arrangements? Who will care?

Sound a little morbid? It's more about being practical. When you live alone and work at home, as I do, interactions with other people are more by choice than schedule. I communicate with most of my clients by email and, occasionally, by phone or text. Most of them are in different cities, or even countries, and I rarely see them in a face to face situation. Ditto for the two people who work with me and are part of my project team. One lives in Illinois, the other in Pennsylvania. We rarely see each other (I see one every three years and have met the other person only twice in person), but we are usually in touch in some way almost every day. Despite that contact, however, they might not think much of it if I disappeared from the radar for a week or so. I often go off on little trips and they might not email or call to check on my status.

You don't have to work from home to find yourself in a similar situation. Anyone who lives alone has wondered what would happen if they died while in the house alone. The older we get, the more we tend to worry about things like this. An entire industry has sprung up selling electronic monitors and alerts that notify emergency responders through a call center that we've 'fallen and we can't get up'. But what if you never have a chance to press the alert button?

The woman who has worked with me for more than 20 years also lives alone and works from a home office in a remote part of Illinois. We have an agreement where we check in with each other periodically to make sure that all is well. Social media such as Facebook are also making it easier to keep track of friends and family. If someone whom we regularly see online stops posting, or if a friend whom we text or chat with fairly often is unheard from, we should check in with them to see how they are. It has never been easier to stay in touch with people or to reach out and connect. This is the positive side of social media.

If you live alone, make sure that you reach out to people regularly, and that you also check on the loved ones in your orbit. This isn't advice for solo people, but common sense for anyone who lives alone. It's also one reason why creating and maintaining a sense of community is so important, even if you are a sworn introvert. Get on someone's radar and stay there. It could save your life in an emergency.

An emergency is also the worst time to be making major decisions. This is especially true when it comes to healthcare decisions that could involve life-extending procedures or other extraordinary measures. If you've ever been in that situation with a family member, you know how difficult it can be, impossible really, to know what to do in a situation where the patient is unable to speak for him or herself.

My mother, my two brothers and I had to deal with a situation like this when my father ended up in the hospital 16 years ago after repeated heart problems, diabetes and kidney failure finally got the best of him. He was essentially in a coma, on life support, and the doctors asked us what we wanted them to do. There wasn't an advanced directive on file and Dad couldn't speak for himself. The prognosis wasn't good. If they turned off the support and he somehow survived, his quality of life would have been very, very low at best. It was a tough decision for the family to make. I knew that he would have hated a 'life' like that and didn't want him to suffer because no one wanted to step forward and make the decision to let him go. No one ever wants to have to make a decision like that.

An advanced directive makes it clear what the patient would want to happen and provides a procedure, usually by naming a healthcare proxy or advocate, to carry those wishes out. It is typically a series of directions provided for a friend or family member to follow in the event that a person is unable to direct the course of his or her own healthcare, such as stroke, dementia or life-threatening illness or injury. Without an advanced healthcare directive in place, the people who care about us can be left scrambling to decide how to move forward with treatment options. A directive can be highly specific regarding treatments (e.g. blood transfusions or organ donations). Often they address life support and 'extraordinary measures' in situations where there in little to no indication that normal function will return, and designate an individual who will ensure that the directive is carried out or make any additional medical decisions on the person's behalf. In today's healthcare climate, that also means giving that person authority under the federal Health Insurance Portability and Accountability Act (HIPAA) so that he or she has access to your medical records. Choosing who to give that authority to is a very important decision. Beyond that, a directive is a highly personal document. There are no right or wrong wishes or preferences.

Much like we decide whether or not to become organ donors when we get our first driver's license, it is never too soon to start thinking about what you would want to happen in a medical emergency or other life-altering situation. Estate planning experts advise everyone over the age of majority (18 or 21 in the U.S., depending on your state) to have a healthcare directive (also known as a living will) and a named power of attorney in order to make it as easy and as inexpensive as possible for the people who are left behind. This is especially important for solos. Spouses can make medical decisions on their partner's behalf. Solos and unmarried partners do not have these same legal rights in a medical emergency or end of life situation unless they take action to create them. "A single person needs to draft a durable power of attorney for medical and financial needs in the event that they are incapacitated and unable to speak for themselves," explained Karen Lee, an accredited estate planner in Atlanta.

Disability and long-term care insurance also become more important for solos because there is no spouse to help with covering expenses in the event of incapacity or inability to work. Solos also need to consider who will inherit their assets when they die. If you die without a will (like Prince did in 2016) or an advanced directive, the laws of the state that you live in will prevail. That may or may not coincide with your wishes, either medically or financially. Do not leave those decisions to people who do not know, or care, about what you would really want.

Longer lifespans, the trend toward having fewer children and fragmented families are driving a related trend: The rising tide of 'elder orphans' – Baby Boomers who have no children, spouse or other family member to care for them as they grow older, or to serve as an advocate for their needs in an emergency. A May 2016 study by Dr. Maria Torroella Carney, the chief of Geriatric and Palliative Medicine at North Shore-LIJ Health System, reported that nearly 25 percent of Americans over the age of 65 are currently at risk of becoming elder orphans. That percentage is likely to increase. According to U.S. Census data, one-third of Americans between the ages of 45 and 63 are single and, as I discussed earlier, the chances of becoming solo again tend to increase as we grow older. In other words, the 'elder orphan' issue is something that everyone should be thinking about and potentially planning for.

Dr. Carney's advice for adults who are in their 50's and 60's and still healthy? Starting making plans for the future now. "Think about advanced directives, get a health care proxy, find an advocate and create a strategy for yourself," she advises.

There are considerable benefits to creating healthcare directives and tackling end of life planning while still young. A 2016 review article on advanced care planning reported that patients who plan in advance for the end of their lives (or a major medical emergency) spend less time in the hospital, receive fewer intensive treatments and have a higher quality of life during their final days. Their surviving relatives and loved ones also experience less stress, anxiety and depression throughout the process. Despite these benefits, only 20 to 30 percent of Americans have put their healthcare wishes in writing in the form of a living will or other legal document.

Patients may not receive the care they want even when an advanced directive is in place due to common errors in the planning process. Putting off making decisions and formalizing a directive due to age ("I'm too young") or good health ("I'm not sick") can be disastrous. Making choices for end of life care is more difficult in the midst of a health crisis. Some preferences, such as avoiding resuscitation, may not be possible if they are not in writing before an emergency occurs. Create a plan now. You can always update your wishes in the future.

It is also important to choose the right person to act as your healthcare proxy when you cannot speak for yourself. Some friends or family members may be overwhelmed with their own grief or guilt and unable to carry out your wishes. Choose someone who you know will have the strength to defend your wishes against the medical system or family members. They don't have to agree with your choices, but they should agree to act as your advocate.

If you have a regular doctor, make sure that s/he has a copy of your directive on file. I carry a copy of my living will in my car, and have other copies in my desk, my safe and my safety deposit box. I am also registered with the Arizona Advanced Directives program, which is a free service offered through the Secretary of State's office. I carry an Advanced Directive card in my wallet which tells first responders and hospital personnel that I have a legal advanced directive on file with the state. Your state may offer a similar program.

It's also important to share your wishes with your loved ones so that they aren't surprised in an emergency and can better support your wishes. According to a survey conducted by The Conversation Project, 90 percent of Americans believe that it's important to discuss end of life wishes with their loved ones, but less than 30 percent have actually had such a conversation.

Your choices may also change as you grow older and new health challenges crop up. Review your directive regularly to make sure that it accurately reflects your current wishes.

After the Curtain Falls

Healthcare is only one aspect of good estate planning. Having a will is another. Unless you have a will in place at the time of your death, your estate will be distributed according to the laws of the state that you live in. If you are married, it will usually pass to your spouse. If you are not, what happens next will depend a lot on where you live.

This is a book about planning for retirement and for life as an older solo adult. This also includes planning for end of life needs. Keep in mind that *everyone* has the potential to become solo at any time. Even if you are married with an estate plan in place, your circumstances will change when your spouse passes. It is proactive and practical for every adult to consider their estate planning needs from a solo perspective. It is likely that, even if you are not solo right now, you will be again at some point in the future.

I am not an estate planner or a financial advisor, but I am a single business owner and homeowner whose children are grown and gone. I have done my homework to help ensure that my wishes will be carried out when I die. For me, that means having an updated will and an advanced healthcare directive in place and on file with my executor. My advanced directive is also on file with the Secretary of State's office in the state where I live. I want to be sure that my final wishes will be carried out.

If you die single and without a will (intestate), your assets will normally pass along bloodlines, first to children, if you have any, and then to your parents, siblings or more distant relatives. If no living relatives can be found, everything that you have worked for may pass to the state where you live. I can't imagine that many people have spent their lives working and saving so that they can leave all of their assets to the state when they die.

Unmarried partners, close friends or charities that you may have wanted to benefit would be out of luck. Many solos are involved in their communities and have causes that are important to them. It makes sense that many of them would want to remember their favorite projects or non-profits in their wills. Having a detailed will in place which designates how money and property should be distributed is the only way to ensure that your wishes are carried out. It will also help ensure that your estate is divided among your children or loved ones according to your wishes, and not theirs.

It is important to appoint an executor to act on your behalf to ensure the fulfillment of your will. Without one, those responsibilities could fall to a distant relative or to a stranger appointed by the state. The decision can be harder for solos who don't have spouses or children to fill this role. The bottom line is that you should always choose the one person whom you trust the most, and implicitly, to carry out your wishes without hesitation or guilt, regardless of whether they are related to you or not. Relatives can find it hard to separate that commitment from guilt or, sadly, greed. An objective unrelated party whom you know well and who knows your preferences first hand may be your best bet.

Keeping beneficiaries up to date on individual retirement accounts, life insurance and bank or investment accounts is also critical. Benefits will likely pass to the people named on these accounts regardless of what your will says. If you are divorced and you do not update your beneficiaries, your ex-spouse could end up with part of your assets. If someone whom you have listed as a beneficiary to one or more of your accounts dies, your assets could pass to their estate. The best strategy is to review your will, your healthcare directive and your beneficiaries regularly. We sometimes remember things differently than they really are, or mistakenly think that we have updated a legal document when we never actually got around to it. Schedule an annual review.

The above represents the basics at best. A successful estate plan fulfills an individual's wishes and works to minimize the taxes owed when they die. Everyone's situation is different. At the same time, everyone – solo or otherwise – needs to be proactive to plan for their future healthcare and estate needs. What's the old saying? There are only two things that are certain in life: death and taxes. Likely there's also a third: the probability that you will end up in a medical situation (e.g. Alzheimer's) where you may not be able to make decisions on your own behalf regarding your medical care or living situation. It's wise to consult an estate planning professional to make sure that you and your wishes will be well represented on all fronts.

Which brings us to the topic of end of life. It's going to happen. Each of us is going to die. Many of us will die solo – some after lifelong single status or decades of being solo; others following the death of a long or short-term spouse or partner. Most of us have preferences for what we want to happen after we pass. Now is the time to also make those wishes known.

One way to help ensure that your wishes are carried out is to pre-plan your own funeral arrangements. There is no guarantee that your family will do things the way that you would like them to be done, even if you share your wishes with them. Including those wishes in your will is one way to take care of the major issues (e.g. burial versus cremation). Your funeral (or lack thereof) wishes can be as detailed or as general as you like. The more specific you are, the more likely you are to end up with the end of life plan you prefer.

Planning ahead will also relieve stress for the people you leave behind, who won't be forced to make decisions and choices, or bear unexpected expenses, during a time of grief. Whatever you choose to do, be sure that it's meaningful to you and not based on what you think you should do, or what other people want you to do. There are very few practices that are required by religion or law. It is your preferences that matter regarding the choice between cremation and burial, embalming (which is rarely required by law), viewing, whether the body is present at the service, or where (or whether) to hold the service in the first place.

Pricing can vary widely for services among funeral homes and other providers. Federal law requires funeral homes to provide price quotes over the phone and a printed, itemized price list when you show up in person. Most experts advise against pre-paying for funeral arrangements. The money you pay now won't be available for emergencies in the future. You may also move or change your preferences, often without being able to get a refund. The money you spend today may not cover future funeral costs, which could result in use of less expensive materials or requests for additional money from your survivors. You might die out of town, or the company you pay could go out of business. The best strategy is to make decisions about what you prefer, put them in writing and then share them with people you trust so that they are available when needed. Send a copy to your executor and others who are close to you, and keep one with a copy of your advanced healthcare directive.

As we get older, many of us also begin to think more about the type of legacy that we will leave behind. The definition of legacy is different for everyone. It could be a project or accomplishment which leaves the world, our community or someone's life in a better state than we found it, or something that we create or build that will continue producing benefits long after we are gone.

I believe that most people want to feel as if they have left their mark on the world in some way that goes beyond creating family, children, or even financial success. Maybe that's just the idealist in me, but I find it hard to believe that I was put on this earth just to get married, have children and build a career and a company. That may be short-selling my accomplishments or my impact on other people, but I am very much focused on creating some kind of legacy which will both outlive me and benefit others. I want to make a difference. I like to think that we all do.

As I get older, I have come to realize that time is precious and that the years are passing faster than ever. Even though I am healthy and active enough that, by most formulas, I should live another 30 to 40 years, I really feel like 'time is of the essence'. In the past year alone, I have increased my pro bono work for organizations and projects that I am passionate about, stepped up my volunteer hours and dedicated more time to writing books on topics that can help others navigate life and work challenges by sharing what I have learned or experienced. I have also begun working with re-careering or recently retired individuals and former executives to help them become 'encore entrepreneurs' who start successful new businesses or consultancies. I am very much in the 'give back' phase of my life (though this has always been important to me). Solos tend to be very community-minded and retirement often provides more time for them to focus on projects which they are truly passionate about. I fit the profile pretty neatly when it comes to this. I have always been other-directed and active in the community. Hopefully, you have a similar inclination, whether you are solo or partnered.

Are you looking to create something that will outlast you? Think about what inspires you and how you can offer that inspiration to others. You may have financial resources that could help fund programs or services that benefit others. Only you can decide what (or who) is important to you and what the best use of your money may be. For those of us who are solo and childless (or essentially childless if our children are gone or out of our lives for some reason), creating a foundation or utilizing planned giving to benefit a favorite organization or cause can be a way to create a legacy that provides benefits to others for many years to come.

Each of us must decide how we want our assets, the fruits of our life's work, our intellectual property and our passions to be passed on. Again, there are no right or wrong answers or wishes. Whether we are solo or partnered, our final wishes and the legacies that we create represent our last opportunity to leave the world a little better than we found it.

APPENDIX

Create a Solo Retirement Plan

It is essential to create a solo retirement plan, even if you don't 'plan' to be on your own in the future. No matter how happily you may be paired at the moment, it is highly likely that you or your spouse or partner is going to end up solo again at some point. Couples who die at the same moment, or even within months of each other, are very rare. You are not being disrespectful to your current relationship, whatever form it may take, to consider and plan for a solo future. Rather, you are being practical and proactive by developing a plan, and your partner should be doing the same.

My journey to create a solo retirement plan for myself and to ultimately write this book actually began by starting to develop an 'un-retirement' plan. I was 57 and entering a time in my life when I wanted to rebalance my life, to make more time to write, travel and explore other avenues and activities that I had set aside while I built and then ran a business, raised a family and worked diligently to put money away for college funds and then, later, retirement. I knew that I never wanted to fully retire. I love what I do, have found a way of doing it that fits my life perfectly and I foresee always being active in my field in some way. I knew that I would feel better (aka 'more secure') if I also had a continuing income stream of some kind. I knew that I wanted more time for me, and that I was in a position to start shifting my priorities to make that possible. My initial goal was to create a balance that dedicated 50 percent of my time to work or professional activities, and 50 percent to 'life' (non-work). You could argue that making more time to write could fall on either side of that mix in my case, but I wanted more time to be able to write for me, under my name, and not just for my clients or my pro bono projects. It was also important to me to be able to live well without drawing on my retirement savings, and to be able to keep that up as long as possible. I had already decided that I was not going to claim Social Security until age 70, if possible, to maximize my future monthly benefit.

My goal was to ease toward retirement by shifting the way that I spend my time. I knew that doing this would likely reduce my annual income, potentially significantly, so I went on to ask and answer these questions for myself:

- How much income would a 50/50 life like this require?

- How could I earn money to achieve that income?

- How would I have to reduce my current expenses to live within that lower income level?

- How and where would I live?

- What would I have to do or change to achieve this lifestyle?

- What are the steps that I need to take to make it happen?

Enter the whiteboard exercise, where I sat down and tried to answer 'what would un-retirement look like' by listing ways that I could continue to earn some income ('make money') while also freeing more time for things that I really want to do ('have more fun'). In my case the potential ways to earn income included consulting for new clients, starting a new business, advising encore entrepreneurs or SBDC clients, writing books and e-books for money, joining a startup as its marketing expert, teaching, coaching speakers or authors, buying a business, getting a part-time job, and selling products or services online. I should add that the easiest way to achieve my financial goal would probably be to do exactly what I am doing now, but less of it, *if* the only goal was to work less. It's not. I also wanted to find new ways to apply and put my expertise and experience to work (which is fun and fulfilling for me), while leaving plenty of time to travel and write. I have always thought of my life as a work in progress and a continuing evolution.

I went on to get more specific by using a branching exercise. A branching exercise puts the goal in the center (solo retirement/un-retirement) and adds branches from that central goal for each of the potential strategies or paths that could be utilized to realize it (e.g. find new clients, find a teaching job, outline my next book, build a website and monetize it, etc.). Smaller branches are then added for the steps that would be needed to achieve each of those individual strategies. A branching exercise forces you to think through the steps to make a plan a reality. For that reason alone, it is priceless. It also helps you visualize the complexity of each of your potential choices. That can help simplify the decision-making process.

Two things became apparently immediately: I already possessed almost all of the skills, expertise or other resources that I would need to be able to pursue any of these paths. I just had to put the 'pieces' that I already had together in different ways. In my case, my list of possibilities was clearly driven by things that I was already experienced in and passionate about – mostly because these pursuits had already touched my life in some way in the past. Whether that was intentional (I always had the interest so I found the outlet) or serendipitous (I was introduced to a new interest through a path that I followed at some point in my life), the result was the same: I was using my life and work experience as building blocks for my future. That's usually a good start.

The other realization was more eye opening: I realized that I am, in many ways, already 'un-retired'. I work very hard at what I do, but my time is my time and I have always had a great deal of flexibility in my schedule. I have worked hard, earned a good living for most of my career and always been careful with my money. With the exception of certain weeks each month, when recurring meetings and client commitments take precedence, or certain months, when recurring projects require my attention, my time is mostly my own to schedule and I am, for the most part, working only about 20 to 25 hours per week, on the average. I was essentially 'un-retired'. I had, however, never given myself permission to use my extra time to write more books, or to devote time to working with aspiring entrepreneurs in a one-on-one setting. I typically spent most of my 'free time' working to drum up more business (more busy-ness?), instead of allowing myself to shift my work/life balance. This was a turning point for me. I was ready and able to shift the balance. *I just had to give myself permission to do so.*

I am, and always have been, a project manager at heart. Project managers love to plan, and they do so by breaking even the most complicated project down into manageable bits. I knew that I needed a plan to make my transition to un-retirement and, at some point, to a more traditional retirement, work. The plan should have a cost attached to it (living expenses), a way to pay for those costs and a strategy to make sure that my primary goal of a 50/50 work/life balance was being met.

I started by creating a worksheet that captured my current living expenses, so I could see how much money I was spending each month and identify areas where expenses could be trimmed if my income was reduced. I knew that I might be able to lower my expenses by buying a home versus renting (depends on the market you live in), or by choosing to live with a housemate (not a preferred option, but a fallback plan). I also knew that there was plenty of room to reduce my monthly credit card use. At the same time, I also knew that some of my costs were likely to go up, particularly healthcare. My monthly premiums go up each year and I am very healthy. Any change in that status could increase them dramatically.

Using the same expense categories, I went on to create a potential un-retirement budget, which would reflect a lower income and, hopefully, lower cost of living. The basic household expenses included rent (or mortgage), utilities, cell phone, internet and cable TV. My monthly expenses also include groceries, going out to eat, hair appointments, health, home and car insurance, and my monthly credit card expenses (which I pay off in full each month). I added a monthly cost for tax deposits (I am self-employed and have to pay quarterly federal and state estimates) and a monthly travel budget (one of my key un-retirement goals).

The total of these expenses told me what I needed to earn on a monthly and an annual basis, gross (before taxes), if I wanted to be able to live that way. I created two versions: one with the monthly travel budget and one without it. The plan with the travel budget became the goal. That gave me a number (my target annual income) to achieve. I was ready to begin planning.

I made a list of the ways that I could earn money to achieve that income goal. I thought about how I wanted to live and where, which helped me decide whether it made more financial sense to rent or buy (I ultimately decided to buy again). My goals in deciding where to live included lots of sunshine, access to a variety of outdoor activities and cultural events, low taxes, affordable real estate costs and proximity to an international airport and other professionals like myself. Your parameters are likely different. I decided to stay in Arizona (which really is a pretty perfect place to live).

I thought a lot about what I wanted my life to look like. For me, the ideal scenario has me experiencing un-retirement (I sometimes call it pseudo-retirement) without retiring completely or drawing on my capital. My quality of life goals included continue to work on interesting projects, meet new people, build a greater sense of community and a stronger social life, expand my outdoor activities, gain new skills and knowledge, and make more time to travel and write. I also have financial goals, which include preserving capital, delaying Social Security and continuing to fund retirement as much as possible, and for as long as possible.

I needed a timeline. A goal with a date become a plan. I knew that I could effectively implement my plan at any time, but I chose September 2016 as the 'official' start date, when I was scheduled to move into my new home. At press time, I was on schedule to meet that goal.

I was (and remain) excited and optimistic. The project manager in me has also considered 'worst case scenarios'. What if I couldn't achieve my new income goal through a 50/50 rebalancing? It was apparent that I was already living an un-retirement type of lifestyle, but I knew that I could always 'go back to work' by finding new clients and projects for my existing company, or by starting a related business. Yes, I know that this is a unique position to be in, but the universal lesson is this: If you were successful in your work life, you will find a way to be successful in retirement. If you were a hard worker and a problem solver before you retired, you are likely to approach the challenges of your new lifestyle in the same way.

Sometimes even the best laid plans don't pan out. If my rebalancing strategy doesn't work out the way that I have planned, I can refine it (likely), abandon it for the time being and go back to work, at least part-time (unlikely), or reshape it completely and accelerate in another direction (always a possibility, which is not necessarily a bad thing). After all, being flexible and 'going with the flow' is what retirement is supposed to be all about.

Worksheets

Solo or otherwise, the entire planning process has to begin by documenting your current assets. You have to know what you have now in order to determine how far you are from your financial goals.

For me this meant creating an Excel spreadsheet, which I update twice a year and send to my younger brother, who is the executor of my estate. This is an important point. Documenting your assets, in detail, will also make it easier for your executor, partner/spouse or other survivors to know what your financial assets are and how to find them. If you are worried about what will happen to your money when you are gone, take the time to document it now – and to update that accounting regularly – to ensure that your assets are not lost or absorbed by the system.

The spreadsheet that I set up is very simple. Across the top, I have columns for Account Location (company/location), Type of Account (e.g. SEP, IRA, non-retirement stocks, savings, checking, CD, etc.), Account Number, Current Balance and Date of Balance. When I update my sheet every six months, I add new columns for Balance and Date of Balance, so I can compare the change in the value of my assets going forward. I usually keep 18 months' worth of numbers (three updates) on the sheet at a time in order to see trends.

The vertical axis includes sections by type of account, including Investment Accounts (retirement and non-retirement), Bank Accounts (checking, saving, business, personal), Certificates of Deposit and any other assets, e.g. annuities. I don't have an annuity, but you may have this or other assets to include. I then total all funds before moving on to non-monetary assets.

The big item on my non-monetary asset list is my home. I show the current appraised value, my cost or outstanding liability against it (mortgage) and the expected net difference, or net value. (If you combine this section with the value of your assets and deduct any other liabilities, you will also have a rough calculation of your net worth, which is a handy number to know.)

Other items on my non-monetary asset list include autos (wholesale value), life insurance (I don't carry any other than what comes with my credit cards), cash on hand, safe deposit contents, and jewelry, collectibles or other items of value.

The key is to create a spreadsheet, electronic or handwritten, and begin documenting and tracking your assets and liabilities. It will make it possible to track your progress toward your goals, spot problem investments or expenses, and make it easier for your executor to ensure that your hard-earned assets do not disappear or get passed to the state where you live.

Resources

I would be remiss if I didn't share some of the resources that I discovered while planning to write this book. This is not an exhaustive list, but it will get you started. The internet is a great source of information. These resources will prod you down the 'rabbit hole' and toward your own journey.

AARP Retirement Calculator www.aarp.org/work

AARP www.aarp.org

Bella DePaulo, Social Psychologist, Author and Expert on Singlism www.belladepaulo.com

Calculate Life Expectancy
- www.livingto100.com
- http://media.nmfn.com/tnetwork/lifespan/#0
- http://www.bankrate.com/calculators/retirement/life-age-expectancy-calculator.aspx

Co-Housing Association of the U.S. www.cohousing.org

Encore Business Advisors www.encorebusinessadvisors.com

HuffPost 50 www.huffpost.com/50

Life Reimagined (AARP) www.lifereimagined.aarp.org

National Shared Housing Resource Center www.nationalsharedhousing.org

Next Avenue www.nextavenue.org

Road Scholar www.roadscholar.org

SCORE www.score.org

Small Business Development Centers https://www.sba.gov/offices/headquarters/osbdc/

Social Security Statement www.ssa.gov/mystatement

The Transition Network www.thetransitionnetwork.org

U.S. Small Business Administration (SBA) www.sba.gov

Women in Community Network www.womenlivingincommunity.com

About the Author

Lori Martinek's multi-faceted marketing and management experience has made her a sought-after strategist and consultant. A successful serial entrepreneur who owns an award-winning marketing and public relations firm, an independent publishing company and is an advisor to new and growing companies, Lori knows how to inspire and help her clients create personal and organizational success.

Lori is an accomplished speaker and a consultant and coach to CEOs, small business owners, community leaders and elected officials. She has counseled new and expanding businesses and is a former president, board member and adviser to chambers of commerce, economic development groups and non-profit ventures.

Lori holds a Master's Degree from Northwestern University's prestigious Medill School of Journalism and a Bachelor's Degree in Journalism from the University of Wisconsin - Madison. She has served as a consultant and/or business analyst for SBA-funded Small Business Development Center (SBDC) programs in Alaska, Arizona, Illinois and New Mexico and for Procurement Technical Assistance Programs (PTAP) in Arizona, Illinois and Maryland.

The author built a successful marketing firm from the ground up while raising a family and being active in the community. Lori's other publishing credits include articles on management and marketing for national publications and bylines in metro newspapers. *Be the Bulb!* was her debut book (Herlife Publishing 2009).

You can learn more about Lori at www.edcgrow.com and at www.encorebusinessadvisors.com.

Made in the USA
Coppell, TX
10 June 2021

57230936R00085